MADDER LOVE

MADDER LOVE

Queer Men and the Precincts of Surrealism

Edited by
Peter Dubé

REBEL SATORI PRESS
Hulls Cove, Maine

Cover image: Evergon, *Faerie from Midsummer Night's Dream*, 1997, hologramme. Book design: Sven Davisson/Rebel Satori Press

Quotes on pages 29 and 30 from "Happy Fag" and "If There's a Hell We're Burning" from Jinx Titanic's *Stuporstardom* (Big Dixie, 2007). Used with permission.

Rebel Satori Press
P.O. Box 363
Hulls Cove, ME 04644
Online: www.rebelsatori.com

10 9 8 7 6 5 4 3 2

Library of Congress Cataloging-in-Publication Data

Madder love : queer men and the precincts of surrealism / Peter Dubé, editor.
    p. cm.
   ISBN 978-0-9790838-2-2 (pbk.)
   1. Gays' writings, American. 2. Gays' writings. 3. Gay men--Literary collections. 4. Surrealism (Literature) I. Dubé, Peter
   PS508.G39M33 2008
   810.8'0920664--dc22
                        2008012561

Contents

A QUEER FRAME OF MIND
Some thoughts on queer writing, surrealism and liberated space, by way of an introduction

The mere word 'freedom' is the only one that still excites me. I deem it capable of indefinitely sustaining the old human fanaticism. It doubtless satisfies my only legitimate aspiration. Among all the many misfortunes to which we are heir, it is only fair to admit that we are allowed the greatest degree of freedom of thought. It is up to us not to misuse it. To reduce the imagination to a state of slavery—even though it would mean the elimination of what is commonly called happiness—is to betray all sense of absolute justice within oneself. Imagination alone offers me some intimation of what *can be,* and this is enough to remove to some slight degree the terrible injunction; enough, too, to allow me to devote myself to it without fear of making a mistake (as though it were possible to make a bigger mistake).[1]

---

1   Breton, André, *Manifestoes of Surrealism*, University of Michigan Press, Anne Arbor, 1982 (Richard Seaver and Helen R. Lane, trans.), page 4.

So wrote André Breton in 1924. I read the words over a half-century later and they have stayed with me ever since. So, let me start this short discussion with an unadorned statement of fact. I must dismiss any pretense of scholarly distance concerning the subjects to be discussed here; to do otherwise would be impossible for me. My discovery of surrealism—and the kinds of claims, like the one above, it so often makes—transformed and tormented me.

I stumbled upon the movement in my adolescence, through a circuitous path that wound (and still winds) through some of the dodgier neighborhoods of popular culture. It was not, I admit, an unusual trajectory for a boy faced by both the onrush of his young manhood and the emergence of his artistic—the word is the most serviceable one available—inclinations. I came to it, its ideas and worldview, its practices and products, through the painters first, as so many others have. I saw those landscapes through dazzled eyes: the endless horizons of Tanguy and the teeming worlds of Max Ernst. That was the beginning for me: a glimpse of infinite, volatile, gorgeous other places. Worlds I wanted, but could never get to. Worlds I thought I would have to create for myself if I were ever to land there.

From the artists, I went deeper into the labyrinth of surrealism; I found the writers, the delirious, glittering torrent of words, the poems, the automatic writing and the major statements, those *Grand Grimoires* of the movement: *Nadja, Paris Peasant, Treatise on Style, Capital of Pain, Mad Love*. Nothing could have been a more powerful enchantment; these texts told me that language could change everything. In their pages I learned that the dizzying worlds I glimpsed in the paintings were *already here*, inside this one, waiting to be found. Every page was a revelation, a guidepost leading me deeper into the pulsating maze.

And the further I went, the closer I came to the Minotaur at the heart of all this wonder—André Breton, a figure that both fascinated and repelled me. There was no escaping him. He presided over the birth of the movement and kept its flame alive, with great tenderness, passion, violence all the years of his life. He was a man of great talent and intelligence, enormous (by all reports) charisma, profound conviction, moral rigor, deep radical commitment, terrible stubbornness and inflexibility, an unfathomable strain of the reactionary and a troubling anti-feminism. Most problematic for me personally at the time of my discovery, Breton was, not to put too fine a point on it, a homophobic prick and I was discovering the many interesting complexities of my homosexuality.

ℛ

My coming out transformed and tormented me as well. By a curious coincidence (or, perhaps in keeping with our theme here, an incident of *objective chance*) I began to come out at a time quite close to the one in which I was discovering surrealism, which means when I was rather young and at school. Happily, I did so in a large city with several universities, multiple languages, a vibrant cultural scene and a strong tradition of left-leaning politics. This fortunate confluence of circumstances meant that there was a queer youth group to join—one run by men already active in the (then) radical Gay Lib movement. Those men, some of whom remain friends to this day and all of whom I honor as mentors, were my entry point into *another take* on the passion for radical change. They represented for me the culture of desire gay men had begun to create, one that seemed related—somehow—to that proposed by the Surrealists, but unblinkered by Breton's prejudices.

The movement I was introduced to was committed to liberating desire and sexuality, sought to create new types of social networks, outside the norms of the family and rooted in fairly radical ideas about elective affection, community and friendship. It—daily—rediscovered the hidden spaces of the city and libidinously revivified them. It wanted to change overarching structures to conform more to the need for self-realization—self-creation even—than to an arbitrary idea of productivity. It was informed by the erotic and it was joyous. Needless to say, I loved it.

But even as I was in the midst of my discovery, this strain of liberationist politics was approaching a terrible *detournement*. I caught its final moments of ascendancy, and, though it (like surrealism) still exists in ways both subterranean and somewhat visible, we all know how this part of the story ends: with a gay movement whose principal concerns are marriage and military service. Not quite the *visionary ardor* by which I was thrilled.

༄

Still despite such disappointments, my development as a man and a writer was marked in profound ways by these two radical visions of the world and its possibilities, and it troubled me to acknowledge the contradictions that seemed to exist between them. The more I read, the deeper my discomfort grew. Awareness of Breton's nastiness is widespread and undeniably accurate. The evidence of his homophobia is littered across the historical record; he threatened, for example, to walk out of the now-famous surrealist group discussions on sex if the general tone of support for homosexual activity continued[2]. Still, despite the many

---

2   See the "Second Session" in José Pierre, *Investigating Sex: Surrealist Discussions 1928-1932*, Verso, London & New York, 1992 (Malcolm Imrie, trans.).

issues of its *de facto* "leader," the movement was volatile and diverse. It hosted a wide variety of struggling viewpoints, saw a lot of schism and hurled accusations, and included queers of all kinds. To name just a few: Rene Crevel, Louis Aragon, Claude Cahun, Pierre Molinier. Moreover, in some ways it was *very queer* in its concerns. Consider for a moment that:

- Surrealism was a movement—like the stream of Gay Liberation that most interests us here—*with desire at its very heart.* And;
- Both were self-consciously interested in subjectivity and the *way the mind operates;*
- Finally, the two movements share an interest in the way these things—subjectivity and desire—*affect the world.*

These similarities, though broad, are significant historically, politically, and in terms of the writing that came out of the two movements, and—certainly—in terms of the writing collected here, which this essay is intended to introduce. Let us, therefore, briefly consider them in turn while looking at a few examples.

Surrealism's concern with desire and love is one of its most central motifs, trumpeted from the earliest years of its history. In the 1930's Breton had already pronounced its importance:

I have never ceased to identify the flesh of the being I loved and the snow of the peaks in the rising sun. I have tried only to know the hours of love's triumph, whose necklace I here clasp about your throat. Even the black pearl, the last one, I am sure you will understand what weakness attaches me to it, what supreme hope of *conjuration* I have placed on it. I do not deny that love has a difference with life. I say it should vanquish, and in order to do so, should rise to such a poetic consciousness of itself that every hostile thing it meets should melt in the hearth of its own splendor.[3]

The surrealist writers conceived of desire as primordial, transformational and overpowering. Desire was a force capable of uniting opposites and dissolving oppositions. In their work it was a power that unveiled the marvelous and fueled freedom and revolutionary fervor, both fostering and nourishing a capacity to transform the world. It operated at an almost cosmic pitch and was a filter through which they viewed life's tumult of activity. Few avant-garde movements would produce as much love poetry, or as much pornography (albeit published in secret, unacknowledged—at first—editions.) Among their titles are these: *Liberty or Love!, Irene's Cunt, Libertinage, Mad Love, The Public Rose* and *Love, Poetry...* a rush of dazzlingly erotic incantations and images in their own right, and books in whose pages the cult of passion is taken to its furthest limits.

Breton would dedicate a volume, *Nadja*, to detailing his obsession with a woman (and his shameful treatment of her.) The strange narrative is an account of how his single-minded passion transformed his experience of life and the city of Paris, while provoking a psychic crisis and releasing a parade of odd, and oddly meaningful, coincidences. Other figures around the movement would write books investigating similar themes as well; the "dissident" surrealist (as he is

---

3   Breton, André, *Mad Love,* University of Nebraska Press, Lincoln and London, 1987, (Translated by Mary Ann Caws) page 114-116.

often characterized) Georges Bataille produced astounding erotic texts that develop an idiosyncratic "mysticism" in which the entire universe is conceived of as throbbing with a poetic and erotic energy. A tension he describes as "... the blending and fusion of separate objects. It leads us to eternity, it leads us to death, and through death to continuity."[4]

The surrealists saw love and eroticism as revolutionary, a matter sufficiently important to be a basis for the new way of life they were developing for themselves. Statements such as this underline the point: "...Love demands the sacrifice of every other value: status, family and honour. And the failure of Love within the social framework leads to Revolt."[5]

This belief in the political and personal importance of desire is a trait they can arguably be said to share with the early gay radicals. It is apparent in many seminal queer texts, such as John Rechy's *The Sexual Outlaw*, which argues for the revolutionary significance of promiscuity in opposing conventional morality and repressive legislation. Other writers made even more vehement cases, like this one by Shively:

> Release all the armor and the shackles, open all the pores and holes up for sexual communication. No restraint in any way. Multiple loves—amoeba-like as in orgies at the baths—single couplings, perhaps between subway stops or between classes or on the way shopping. We must be open at all times for sexual activity; in fact not make it an in-between action, but

---

4   Bataille, Georges, *Erotism: Death and Sensuality,* City Lights Books, San Francisco, 1986, (Mary Dalwood, trans.) page 25.
5   The "Manifesto on l'Age D'Or," in André Breton, *What is Surrealism: Selected Writings,* Monad Press, New York, 1978, (Franklin Rosemont, ed.) page 328.

make every action sexual."[6]

The surrealists and the authors of the early radical queer milieu, though operating in different eras and from wildly divergent positions, seem in agreement on some basic assumptions: sexuality, desire, passion are powers in the human psyche and the world, and are valid, important ways in which people connect with each other. They overlap in the conception of desire and love as being capable of disrupting and transforming ordinary relationships, social organization and consciousness.

This last term, the question of consciousness, brings us in some ways to another point of similarity. One finds an active investigation of how the mind actually works and an interest in subjectivity—how it is constructed, displayed, deployed—in the writing of both groups. Though a concern of almost all modernist writing, the surrealist group made mental activity a particularly central part of their creative research. This interest begins with the movement's earliest statements; the first manifesto would launch a definition of surrealism as "psychic automatism in its pure state, by which one proposes to express— verbally, by means of the written word, or in any other manner—the actual functioning of thought."[7] This fascination would extend through much, not to say most, work produced thereafter. Operating from such a focus, surrealist texts would follow the movements of the mind precisely: tracking the twists and leaps in verbal consciousness, the sudden focuses and, contrarily, shifts of attention, the way awareness slides across some things and the paradoxical way in which other things

6   Shively, Charley, "Indiscriminate Promiscuity as an Act of Revolution" in *Gay Roots: Twenty years of Gay Sunshine*, Winston Leyland (ed), Gay Sunshine Press, San Francisco, 1991, page 262 .
7   Breton, 1982, op cit, page 26.

suddenly appear in a flash, freighted with enormous "meaning." They would pursue the concern through their experiments with trance states, automatic writing, the recording and study of dreams, but also through the work they did with their own lives and images (as in the *corpus* of the artist and writer Claude Cahun, for example) a specific practice that connects up with the approaches of many queer creators.

In fact, in some respects, queer authors might have preceded the surrealists in the literary exploration of the nature and activity of the mind (albeit with a somewhat different focus) and although a great deal of prose, historical and contemporary, concerns itself with drawing psychologically compelling portraits, comparatively less of it has so deliberately foregrounded mental activity as a kind of primary content as queer writing. It is possible to speculate concerning the reasons for this; the conjunction of—until quite recently—an awareness that one is psychically *different* from most people with the need for an almost paranoid awareness of the threat of arrest and ostracism might incline one to monitor one's inner life fairly closely, but for our purposes, the textual artifacts themselves are of more immediate concern. From the earliest periods in which it was even possible to hint at "unusual" mental states or inclinations in publicly circulated texts, queers were creating such artifacts. One need only think of the psychologically and textually dense body of work produced by Henry James, which is certainly the most celebrated case and now firmly ensconced in the canon. But there were others delving into the possibilities of cultivating and exploring the psyche, of tracing the impact of impression and sensation as it passes across a consciousness. It certainly required an established context for Walter Pater to write:

To burn always with this hard, gemlike flame, to

maintain this ecstasy, is success in life. In a sense it might even be said that our failure is to form habits: for, after all, habit is relative to a stereotyped world, and meantime it is only the roughness of the eye makes any two persons, things, situations, seem alike. While all melts under our feet, we may well grasp at any exquisite passion, or any contribution to knowledge...[8]

Nor did this queer concern with the nature and possibilities of subjectivity vanish with the turn of the century and the trial of Pater's most famous student, Oscar Wilde. It is a nearly continuous current in what was, until the Sixties, an underground river of gay writing, clearly present in the work of the Beats and their contemporaries. Burroughs' experiments with cut-ups in particular were a self-conscious expansion of the surrealist use of automatism and were undertaken with Brion Gysin, who had briefly been associated with the surrealist group, providing a vital historical link between the two traditions of writing. During the same period, the aforementioned John Rechy's writing appeared, containing vivid passages that suggest a related exploration of subjectivity. The opening of his *City of Night* is telling:

> Later I would think of America as one vast City of Night stretching gaudily from Times Square to Hollywood Boulevard—jukebox-winking, rock-n-roll moaning: America at night fusing its darkcities into the unmistakable shape of loneliness.
>
> Remembering Pershing Square and the apathetic

---

8   Pater, Walter, *The Renaissance*, The Modern Library, New York, no date provided, page 197.

palmtrees. Central Park and the frantic shadows. Movie Theatres in the angry morning-hours. And wounded Chicago streets... Horrormovie courtyards in the French Quarter—tawdry Mardi Gras floats with clowns tossing out glass beads, passing dumbly like life itself... Remembering rock-n-roll sexmusic blasting from jukeboxes leering obscenely, blinking manycolored along the streets of America strung like a cheap necklace from 42nd Street to Market Street, San Francisco ...

One-night sex and cigarette smoke and rooms squashed in by loneliness...

And I would remember lives lived out darkly in that vast City of Night, from all-night movies to Beverly Hills mansions."[9]

Here the sense of a mind moving across experience is palpable; slight details loom large, defining whole cities, entire relationships. One feels an intimacy with the narrative voice, tracking its own processes from the initial statement "I would think" that establishes the tone of everything to fellow: "think," "remember," "remembering" are the operative verbs in the passage, setting all the lavish imagery within a space of subjectivity. Words are compounded, "darkcities" and "manycolored" among them, whose unexpected marriage suggests the breakneck speed of consciousness, an evocation given almost irresistible force by the prose rhythms. Time and space and the travel across or through them are condensed, displaced and mirrored in the tension between a fluid narrative consciousness and the concrete specificity of language.

---

9   Rechy, John, *City of Night*, Grove Press, New York, 1963, page 9.

Rechy's catalogue of places and their emotional and psychic impact takes us to the third point in this (necessarily partial) catalogue of cross-fertilizations. From the mechanics of the mind in itself, we pass to the ways and means by which such subjectivity interacts with, permeates and shapes our lives and the world; a theme, which, in a sense, synthesizes the two others. Taking the mind and its functioning along the vector of desire must, necessarily, demonstrate that mind's *relationship to something*. One of the principal areas explored by the Surrealist Group for such a relationship lies in their ideas about the dream.

A model of dream and reality as interdependent and overflowing into one another is the central focus of Breton's *The Communicating Vessels*. In that book long, winding sentences move from dream images to paintings, from women encountered on the street to those in his imagination. Signs and significances erupt around him as the author moves through his days. It is a book in which, in the words of critic Mary Anne Caws, "Breton shows at some length, the relation of his own dreams to everyday life, the similar structure in each, and how each works towards the 'reconstitution' of himself..."[10] which is to say who he is and how he operates in life—the ways in which dream and waking life have an equal part in *constructing us*.

However, the theme of the mind's relationship to some *other*, of the overlap of physical and psychic life, would be considered by the Surrealists in ways more far-ranging than the correspondences between dream life and waking activity, regardless of how compelling that puzzle would remain for them. The investigation would be extended to the relationship of interior life to the world's physicality itself, its blunt

10 Caws, Mary Ann, "Linking and Reflections: André Breton and his Communicating Vessels," in *André Breton Today*, Anna Balakian and Rudolf E. Kuenzli (eds), Willis Locker & Owens, New York, 1989, page 93-94.

facts, and—more often than not—to the city and the urban landscape. The surrealists' practice of aimless wandering through Paris' streets and arcades, their endless hunts through the flea markets in search of some numinous trinket provides a key illustration of this concern in the group's daily activities, but it also occupies a prominent place in surrealist writing. Aragon offers a particularly potent statement of the way in which the mind and the city interact in his *Paris Peasant*:

> The whole fauna of human fantasies, their marine vegetation, drifts and luxuriates in the dimly lit zones of human activity, as though plaiting thick tresses of darkness. Here, too, appear the great lighthouses of the mind, with their outward resemblance to less pure symbols. The gateway to mystery swings open at the touch of human weakness and we have entered the realms of darkness. One false step, one slurred syllable together reveal a man's thoughts. The disquieting atmosphere of places contains similar locks which cannot be bolted fast against infinity.[11]

Aragon's readiness to slide across the dividing lines between a street or a building and the world of human thought or the symbolic order points to a key iteration of surrealist ideas about the interplay of world and mind. Here bricks and mortars take "reality," which is to say meaning, through the way in which they respond to, or resonate with, the people moving among them; the way in which they reflect and play out within the arena of their desires. Aragon tackles these themes

---

11 Aragon, Louis, *Paris Peasant*, Exact Change, Boston, 1994 (Translated by Simon Watson Taylor) page 13.

through skewed, detailed meditations on shop windows and the signage of bars. In his carefully constructed paragraphs he demonstrates, with a precision that is almost an embodiment, the dialogue between things and the *experience* of things. The surrealist landscape becomes, in short, a living place—a kind of relationship.

Queer men too have hymned the city and the multifarious life to be found there, writing exceptionally evocative statements about the erotics of streets and parks, subway platforms and alleys. The literature of cruising, for example, is to a significant extent as much about an *experience of time and place* as it is about sex. Edmund White, in his extraordinary *Nocturnes for the King of Naples*, writes of time spent in the old piers:

> A wind said incantations and hypnotized a match flame up out of someone's cupped hands. Now the flame went out and only the cigarette pulsed, each draw molding gold leaf to cheekbones.
>
> There are qualities of darkness, the darkness of gray silk stretched taut to form the sky, watered by city lights, the darkness of black quartz boiling to make a river, and the penciled figures of men in the distance, minute figures on—is that a second story? What are they doing up there? A cigarette rhymes its glow with my own across the huge expanse that has shattered its crystal lining to the ground.[12]

The passage underlines the mutual permeability of perceiver and

12 White, Edmund, *Nocturnes for the King of Naples*, Penguin Books, New York, 1980, pages 1-2.

perceived during the act of observation; the figure takes on a gold that is purely imaginary, the river becomes boiling black quartz in an act that is at once lived experience and takes place entirely mentally. The intensity of the language (which coincidentally enough echoes something of Aragon's concern with varieties of darkness and the way in which they speak to interior life) is given additional power through the longing it both contains and performs, reflecting the eroticism of a place and the infinitely mutable encountering of it. It reveals the way in which the perceiver *takes part* in place itself in a way that strikingly parallels much of the surrealists' writing, making of these two traditions, too, a series of "communicating vessels"; creating a landscape throbbing with desire, a vividly self-conscious universe that seems alive, and endlessly fornicating. As Annie Lebrun, a contemporary surrealist suggests:

> If there is such a thing as a surrealist revolution, it is inseparable from the affirmation of desire as a physical intuition of the infinite.[13]

And there are moments in queer life (and art) of which much the same could be said.

෨෩

At this juncture, it would be pertinent to point out that LeBrun's comment has additional significance deriving from the fact that it is made by a contemporary surrealist; it underlines that surrealism remains a living tradition. Despite the eagerness on the part of official literary

---

13 LeBrun, Annie, "Desire—A Surrealist 'Invention'" in *Surrealism: Desire Unbound,* Mundy, Jennifer (ed), Princeton University Press, Princeton, 2001, page 308..

and art history to embalm the movement (and regardless of the dispute about the exact date it "ended:" World War II, the death of Breton in 1966, etc.), the fact is that many are still very much concerned with the central surrealist issues, and continue exploring them with or without a critical *imprimatur*. There are numerous contemporary writers (of all sorts of sexual and identity categories) publishing who make no secret of their surrealist interests and/or affiliations; nor did the particular kind of literary exploration of subjectivity done by queer authors, discussed above, stop mid-century. That tradition, too, continued in the post-Stonewall era and down into our own day. One can see it in the work of the "Violet Quill" group whose tracing of the psychic vagaries of life in the gay ghetto and the psychological stakes of self-presentation are deeply textured by attention to phenomenological detail. One can trace a line (although wandering) from them to someone as distant from their immediate concerns as Dennis Cooper whose investigations of psychological states, particularly extreme ones, and the fine line between "fantasy" and "reality" owe some debt to the nineteenth and turn-of-the century writers[14] already referenced, and which could be linked to at least a few of the concerns of surrealism. Of note in this regard too is the recent novel *Skin Lane* by Neil Bartlett, a writer whose interest in such precursors to surrealism as the Symbolists is well established. In that narrative, the handsome young man who is the object of the protagonist's desire makes a seemingly literal transition from the realm of dreams to the actual flesh and blood world.

Though the continued vibrancy of surrealism, "official" and "unofficial" alike, and the whole range of queer writing pleases me

14 An interesting investigation of such a debt can be found in James Annesley's "Contextualizing Cooper" published in Leora Lev (ed.), *Enter at Your Own Risk: The Dangerous Art of Dennis Cooper*, Fairleigh Dickinson University Press, Madison/Teaneck, 2006.

mightily, it was the submerged parallels between them that formed and informed my intellectual, literary and political life for so many years. That sheer staying power lead to the suspicion that what had so long fascinated me might have equal power for other queer men, other queer writers. I was haunted by the possibility that other people were roaming the nexus of queerness and surreality in *deliberate* ways. I wanted to know if there were any such.

Well, there were. That exploration is precisely what the writers collected here are doing; these texts take the *influence* of surrealism and call back, responding to it as a form of mental adventure, or harmonizing with its focus on desire and the marvelous, or tracing the living activity of the mind, but regardless of the details each of them are aware of the ground on which they've staked their claim. They set out and explore those rich, provocative and radical overlapping worlds with some remarkable results. They clamor for the marvels that lie just beyond—or buried inside—what we see everyday, and they manage to unveil them just a little, each in his own particular way.

Which brings me to a few *caveats*. This book is emphatically *not intended* to be an anthology of *"queer surrealists"* as such—hence the qualifier of the subtitle. The writers collected here may or may not so designate themselves, (to be honest it wasn't a criterion for selection, and I never asked, because that is not the point of the book). *Madder Love* is intended, rather, to look at the way certain themes, concerns, points of view and kinds of literary "material" are common to both literary traditions, and the way in which these resonances affect contemporary writing. Surrealism is, therefore, given its widest possible sense in this book. For that reason some of the work contained here may appear more or less "surreal" at first glance; however, it will undoubtedly prove useful to the reader to bear in mind the truest sense of the "sur" in surrealism as meaning a step beyond ordinary perception, and one can as easily reach for that other place by burrowing through the surface of the real as by stretching it out.

Also, I did not fuss over the well-policed borders of genre while reading submissions. *Madder Love* contains a rich diversity of material that will trouble easy categorization. It also, I'm delighted to say, contains work by writers who are equally difficult to classify—publishing work that might generally be regarded as more "literary" on one hand, or more "genre" focused on the other. I believe there is interesting—and excellent—work being done on both sides of that increasingly difficult to maintain boundary and surrealism's influence is felt as much in popular culture as it is in the halls of the academy or the slopes of any self-proclaimed Parnassus. At any rate, such generic divisions are deeply contested, theoretically suspect and of dubious critical value.

I should note as well that I have chosen to focus on men in this anthology simply because that is the literary tradition with which I am most familiar as a writer and an editor. Given the presence of queers of all kinds in both the original surrealist group and related activity since then, there are undoubtedly similar books to be made in relation to women and others, and I encourage those with the necessary expertise to take up the challenge. I will certainly be among such titles' readers if, and when, they appear. Finally this book anthologizes prose and hybrid forms of writing, largely because there have already been several anthologies exploring surrealist-informed poetry.

Looking back now to when I first issued the call for submissions for *Madder Love,* I remember thinking to myself how strange the underlying concept might appear to readers given Breton's notorious homophobia. A number of friends even emailed me asking about this seeming paradox. But the truth is that the paradox itself is an important part of this project. This book wants to reclaim—in the small ways it can—what is beautiful, complex and untamed in surrealism for queers and to assert what is beautiful, complex and untamed in queerness for surrealism, because both are vital in a world sliding towards a deadening, market-driven homogeneity.

Between these covers are a group of writers whose work (my own contribution aside) illustrates why the intersection of queerness and surrealism remains so rich and so compelling. I am deeply grateful to the authors, because within this writing lies—thanks to their audacity, imagination and willingness to take risks—a little of the freedom that Breton, for all his contradictions, cared for enough to write of with so much passion. And, let us admit that if we can make some small place for freedom of thought and experience even simply in our writing and the stories we tell each other, that is—at least—a good beginning.

I hope you find some measure of it in your reading here today.

Peter Dubé

Epidemic

Stephen Beachy

The boy and his twin live on a street where every family has two sons. The oldest son is always adopted, because the women think they are barren, or they think their men are full of faulty sperm. Either way, as soon as they adopt a boy, the problem corrects itself and they get pregnant. Up and down the street, there are adopted sons cohabiting with the natural born sons of their parents. In every family, one son is effeminate and one son is not. Sometimes the older boy is a big sissy and sometimes the younger boy.

The twins are five. At random intervals, their family receives a visitor from the night: a paperboy. It is always snowing out there in the night, and the paperboy is glorious to behold. The twins cower behind some parent, adoring the paperboy and his temperate skin. Over time they get closer; words are exchanged; they involve the paperboy in brief games and fantastic invitations. One thing leads to another: a fort is constructed of ice and snow. The paperboy has taken time out from his duties—there is just enough room inside for the three of them.

I must go on a long journey, says the paperboy. To stay here and love you would be a crime. To stay here together, our orifices steaming in the cold, would be nothing but crime.

The paperboy uses many vocabulary words the twins don't yet

know. He kisses the twins and speeds off on his snowmobile; the twins can't even remember the older boy's name.

After the snows have thawed, the boy and his twin play in the vacant lot behind their house, a lot full of milkweed and thistle, monarch butterflies and an occasional tiger swallowtail. They capture these butterflies in nets, keep them in jars until they die, and then pin them to a piece of Styrofoam. There are three mounds in this field, and an adjacent garbage dump. They don't know who built the mounds, but can see that whoever did was aware of the 584 day cycle of Venus, through which it appears as the evening star, disappears for a short period and then reappears as the morning star. The rising of the Pleiades also seems to have been taken into account. In this field, the twins invent a game they call "chasing the rabbits". They take off their clothes and display themselves to the garbage men who visit the dump. Some of the garbage men play along, chasing the boys through the weeds, capturing them and taking them into their trucks. The boys' lives are enchantment: every day they are either chasing butterflies or being fondled by garbage men. One day, the boy and his twin follow a shabby moth into the tall weeds of the second mound, and sit for a rest.

That garbage man that caught me yesterday was pretty good, one of them says, But I sure do miss the paperboy.

Remember when he built us that fort? says the other.

I remember the quivering lips, the soft cheeks, the intelligent eyes, and the firm boyish buttocks of the paperboy, one of them says. He was so pedantic, but I loved him.

He was overly controlling, concedes the other one. But aren't they all?

Are we a crime? he says to his twin.

Just then a man drives up on a tractor. Oh no! his brother says. It's the salt-shaker man!

A glazed look comes over him then, as if he is a zombie who has lived freely for many years, for so long that he has forgotten that he is undead and a slave, until his master rides up on a tractor to take him away.

The boy returns home alone and crawls inside a kitchen cupboard, where he remains for several weeks, eating the Hamburger Helper, instant mashed potato flakes, and uncooked Cream of Wheat he finds there. In the cupboard, stunned by the "kidnapping" of his twin, or the voluntary surrender of his twin to some previously negotiated, secret and criminal relationship, the boy hallucinates, in the intricate manner of those simultaneously starved, traumatized, and sensorily deprived, and what he hallucinates is his own future, which he understands to have been previously negotiated, through his secret and criminal relationship with the paperboy, whose name he can't remember; mixed in with extraneous visual cartoons involving an infinity of rivers and canoes or an endless geometric progression of vaguely occult shapes, he hallucinates his own employment in the same profession as his lover, the impending loss of his parents, and his erotic trajectory as an orphan among cult members and insane girls; he hallucinates the endless plains of a foreign country, flat and hazy, the horizon as inscrutable as the pale blue nothingness of sky; and he hallucinates a train crawling across the endless plains without benefit of a conductor. As he hallucinates, he chews on a plastic elephant, which he imagines is a piece of chocolate given him by a sadistic little girl with hair the color of light itself; he hallucinates, in fact, an entire cosmos made of the hair of the sadistic and insane girl, a rippling wig of light which expands geometrically in every direction and causes him nothing but pain.

But he grows older and becomes a paperboy.

He is just a boy and in the sixth grade and he studies hard and never misses a spelling word and one night while he is sleeping, it is winter; a stranger knocks on his bedroom window.

What is the name of this city? the man asks.

The Mazes, the paperboy says. Or the Innards or The Mounds.

But where is the river? the man asks.

I've been there, the boy says. But the directions are complicated.

The man just stares at him.

You aren't the salt-shaker man, are you? asks the boy.

Stop talking gibberish, says the stranger.

He looks familiar, not like the paperboy has known him, but like he is the sort of man everyone means when they say Don't get in the car with a stranger or Don't reveal intimate details to a stranger or Don't take any sweet things from a stranger.

You remind me of someone, says the boy. He was my Language Arts teacher, but he's taken a leave. He was a stern man, but not without a certain charm. He got the most out of me, that's for sure.

I don't give a shit how you spell your words, says the stranger.

OK, says the boy. Then what do you want?

I want to bind you hand and foot, the stranger says.

Is that what you'll do if I let you in?

I was just kidding.

The paperboy expects to see a blinking neon sign outside his window. He feels that he is in a motel. He feels that he has always been in a motel, but didn't realize it until now. Is there blood and excrement smeared on the walls? The boy opens the window.

Later, the stranger leaves him there, drained of his will.

He is an orphan.

After the funeral, an elaborate affair involving many of the city's florists and greeting card manufacturers, the orphan is taken down into the bad part of town behind the warehouses and barely utilized malls, past a parking lot full of old school buses. Through a maze of gravel roads and abandoned industrial equipment and back among the trees, where they are waiting for him with a boat. He is floated down the icy river on the boat and outside of town, where, for the first time in his life, he sees the stars. While his social worker LuAnn apathetically rows him into the unknown, the constellations and the planets fill the sky and their reflection fills the river.

At a farm outside of town, she hands him over to a group of men with long beards, who wade into the river and tie the boat to a post. They lead him into an empty schoolhouse and explain to him the history of their cult. The differences which separated the followers of Jakob Amman from the Swiss Anabaptists centered on the practice of shunning and the strictness of conformity to specific social and ritualistic practices. They speak in perfect English to him and leave him to copy several lists off the blackboard. He hears them just outside the door, speaking now in some harsh, barbaric tongue in time with the distant clip-clop of a briskly trotting horse—a sinister rhythm.

The women of this cult wear lace doilies on their heads. They spend their days quilting—patching together a piece of this, a piece of that, to make something more useful than showy. They eat hamloaf and shoo-fly pie and apple-butter. The two spices used in their cuisine are salt and MSG. The cult members are pacifists who believe that electricity is evil. Tractors with pneumatic tires are another taboo. Their quaint expression for abandoning the *Ordnüng*, the established ways of the cult, is to "go through the red door". They keep only one non-biblical text, a vast book full of pictures of men and women in pain. They don't show him the book, but describe some of the images in detail. A tall, thin man refuses to be a soldier and personal bodyguard for the King of Prussia, because of his religious convictions. Soldiers pinch and thumbscrew this tall, thin man. They hang him from a cord by his left thumb and his great right toe. The orphan believes there are pictures of his murdered parents and his kidnapped twin in that book.

They leave him his electric guitar, but there is no way to plug it in. Meanwhile, he is put to work. The farm is primarily an enormous windowless building crammed full of chickens on various levels. There are rows and rows of wire cages in which chickens are packed together with barely enough room to peck each other. Underneath are troughs, where the eggs gather. It is the orphan's job to enter the building in the morning and the evening, to walk up and down row after row after row, gathering the eggs. The stench is incredible.

Deep in the bowels of the chicken house, he comes face to face with a handsome boy with a crushed, sullen look. This boy is gathering the carcasses of chickens that have pecked themselves to death.

Welcome to the crazy house, the other boy says.

This boy was taken in as a Fresh Air child. Every summer these Fresh Air children are sent out to the religious cult from the city because of a pervasive belief that hard work and clean country living will make them less angry when they grow up, more likely to hold a job and not to steal.

But I've been kept on permanent, the Fresh Air child explains.

I thought I could plant trees here, he says. That's what I thought being a Fresh Air child was all about. But the air here reeks of feathers and shit and all the trees have been chopped down.

Other than the bearded men and the women with lace doilies covering their hair, there is a group of rough boys always wandering the farm, bare-chested and with cowboy hats. They wear tight blue-jean shorts and frolic with a rubber inner-tube in the swimming hole at the edge of the farm. There is a crazy girl locked in the barn.

In the fields, there are cows.

At night the Fresh Air child leads the orphan out to the swimming hole under the light of the full moon, knowing that the rough boys will be out on the country roads speeding through the dust and drinking and doing crystal meth and will not bother them. The orphan brings his useless guitar along, and pretends to play music for a strip-tease. It is absolutely quiet at the swimming hole and the two boys strip to their underwear and splash in the unusually warm water and then lay together on the rocks.

The cows are contained by endless coils of barbed wire. Fragrant vines with tiny white flowers have grown over this barbed wire. In the moonlight, the flowers look like tiny ghosts strung along the walls of a lush dark prison.

Not far from the swimming hole sit the remains of a car accident. Car parts and cow skeletons and other bones which look like they might belong to a boy just about the orphan's size are all mixed up together. A sign has been placed next to the accident or collage, which reads *Der Übel des Beförderungmodern.*

A hex sign hangs on the barn. The crazy girl's name is Beth and she has long hair the color of light itself. I've never seen her, the Fresh Air child says, but I love her just the same. I love her so much, he says, as the orphan touches him too. The orphan climbs up into the hayloft above Beth's compartment, and speaks down to her through the cracks between boards.

Well, well, well, she says. It's the voice from above.

The hayloft is full of dust that dances in the moonbeams that filter in through cracks in the roof. The orphan lights a kerosene lamp. It flickers and stinks.

Does any of the light reach you down there? the orphan asks.

It doesn't have to, Beth says. Studies have proven that light isn't good for insane people.

Didn't you ever read that? asks Beth. Out there in the world?

I love you, says the orphan.

I live here in my own excrement, she says.

You're the most beautiful girl I've ever seen, says the orphan.

That's what they all say.

He fidgets in the hayloft. There are mice and other small rodents, small birds that build their nests in the rafters. The cows are all around, brooding.

Leave me alone now, says Beth.

The orphan goes down to the swimming hole one afternoon during his break between the morning collection of eggs and the evening collection of eggs. He watches the rough boys and their games. Hey orphan shit, they say, what are you looking at? Hey you little piece of faggot paperboy ass, they say, you better stay there on shore or you might get drowned.

They bare their asses at him, accuse him of liking it, and do dangerous dives into the pond.

They sunbathe on the rocks. They discuss raping him. All of the girls out here are hideously ugly, they say, except for Beth and she is insane and locked in the barn. They tell many jokes with punchlines involving butt-sex. They do lines of coke and speed off in their souped-up horse and buggies.

What do you want, voice from above? asks Beth.

I want to understand the relations between people on this farm, the orphan says. I want to know who you are and why you are locked in the barn. I want to know who the rough boys are and their relationship to the religious cult.

She sighs.

The rough boys are the sons of the cult, says Beth. They are given a period of time in which none of the laws of the cult apply to them, called "sowing their wild oats."

And who are you? asks the orphan.

I have something for you, she says. But you have to be very careful with it.

She reaches her hand up toward him and shows him an egg.

I gather eggs all morning and eggs all evening, says the orphan. I dream about eggs and when I wake up everywhere I look is eggs, eggs, eggs.

The last thing I need, says the orphan, is an egg.

Beth tosses it up to him. He catches it and examines it. It looks just like any other egg.

Keep it and watch it, she says. And the most important thing: don't get any blood on it.

What about the red door? asks the boy. Does this have something to do with the red door?

That old thing? says Beth. I'll tell you, I went through that door a long time ago. That door is not all that. That door is not what it's cracked up to be.

And what does *Der Übel des Beförderungmodern* mean? he asks.

The evil of modern transportation, says Beth.

The orphan is altogether lost—more than anything, he loves

modern transportation. More than anything, he loves snowmobiles and garbage trucks and mopeds. He even loves tractors with pneumatic tires. More than anything, he loves the boys and men who drive them, and more than anything, he loves Beth. When he was five, his desires were so clear: the paperboy, the butterflies, and the garbage men. Or was that just what his twin wanted, and he went along for the ride? Now it's even more mixed up, with various rules and humiliations.

One other thing, says the orphan.

Since my twin brother went missing and my parents are dead, the boy says, I'm considered an at-risk youth. Are you an at-risk youth?

The only thing I like about my cult, or family, says Beth, is the quilting. Quilting is all about weaving chaos into barely perceptible patterns with subtle repetitions and geometries. I like to patch together a piece of this, a piece of that, to make something showy and extreme. For obvious reasons, they won't let me have needles; the only quilts I can make are ghostly and ephemeral.

Listen, she says. Since you love me so much, do me a favor. I need more chalkboards and chalk. You'll find stacks of little chalkboards and cartons of chalk in the supply closet of that awful little one-room school-house.

The orphan is confused; he's probably a little bit sleep-deprived. Is that a one-room school-house or a prison? Is it a place of learning or an erotic nightmare? Tortured rote-learning or the pleasures of repression that come with world domination? At night, the cows here begin to cluster around the northern edges of their range. They start biting through the barbed wire and walk on in rapidly expanding herds. North, north. Soon there are no more cows except the veal calves, still trapped in their pens. In the north, beneath the startling lights of the aurora borealis, the cows are trudging on. Snow is falling on the dreaming cows.

If there's one thing these people love, Beth says, it's their chalkboards and their chalk.

The one-room school-house is never locked. Under another full moon, the rough boys draw weird geometrical shapes with chalk in the dirt outside, echoing the vaguely occult designs on the barn's hex sign, and place a veal calf in the center of it, tightly bound with their lassos. They're performing rituals to bring the cows back. The orphan sneaks past them and loads up on supplies. He hides them under the bed where the Fresh Air child is fast asleep and dreaming. The orphan can barely contain his love for the dreaming Fresh Air child. Why would he? He puts the egg under the other boy's pillow.

Back outside, blood is splattering everywhere, the boys going at it with hacksaws and axes. They reach into the warm calf and rip out organs, intestines. The orphan pretends to faint.

The boys, bare-chested and covered with calf's blood, tie him up with their lassos. They tie him up with so much rope that only his quivering lips, his soft cheeks, his intelligent eyes and his firm boyish buttocks remain visible. The long nozzles hang down from their gas masks like the trunks of some reconstituted biotech mammoths from a genetically engineered future. He is bored and delighted. He wonders about the future evolution of life on Earth. He wonders where these pacifist boys get their gas masks.

How's the egg, voice from above? asks Beth.

The egg is fine, says the orphan.

He drops several stolen chalkboards down, and chalk.

Where do you think the cows went? he asks.

I've been strangely napping, she says.

She says, My dreams have been truly bizarre.

Beth disappears. It is reported that she has drowned in the swimming hole. The details are vague. Her footprints clearly lead to the pond but never exit. The pond is red and cloudy. The farm-boys continue to swim there regardless, playing their rough games with the rubber inner-tube.

When he goes to gather the eggs one morning, the boy sees red. The trough is full of bloody eggs, nothing but bloody eggs. He screams and a man with a beard comes running in.

The eggs are all bloody, he says.

There's nothing wrong with these eggs, the bearded man says.

One morning there are only a few eggs in the trough. When he returns in the evening there isn't even one. The chickens have stopped laying.

He is sent to the barn where Beth was housed instead, to clean up her mess. The planks of the walls and floor are covered with blood and excrement. He is dizzy, has a flashback: he's in a motel. When he regains his composure, he cleans. Buried beneath mounds of dried excrement, he finds her chalkboards, on which she has scrawled elaborate stories of abuse in ghostly chalk scribbles. On one chalkboard he finds a list of twenty words, with the first half X'd out. *Effeminate* is X'd out, *eternity* is X'd out. Left over are clenched, unscrupulous, bleached, gnashed, convoluted, eroded, plateau, petroglyph, corroded, epidemic, and sores. Out of the corner of his eye the scrawled words seem to form subtle patterns and non-Euclidean geometries. But then he discovers a note scrawled in lipstick that looks like thick greasy blood: Hey, voice from above, it says. *I am not really dead.*

One of the rough boys grabs him by the throat and drags him up the ladder into the hayloft. Once he has him up there, however, he is gentle, not rough, and he introduces the orphan to a different kind of chore.

I love you more than anything in "the world", the rough boy confesses.

I don't love you, thinks the orphan.

But he likes the rhythm of the chore. The farm-boy really puts his back into it.

I'll tell you a secret, the farm-boy says. They have discovered that the insane girl is not really dead.

Oh, really? says the orphan. He wiggles and shifts his position, as if he could care less about that crazy girl.

She has run off with a preacher, says the farm-boy. A preacher from the Church of Christ with the Elijah Message. An unscrupulous and adulterous man who will surely take advantage of her. She is to be shunned. We shall never mention her name again. We shall pretend she doesn't exist, until she realizes the error and loneliness of her ways.

The bearded men call the orphan and the Fresh Air child into the empty schoolhouse.

We've been carefully monitoring you, they say, for signs of madness and criminality. We love madness and criminality. We're afraid you may be flirting with the idea of pneumatic tires on your tractors.

We are perfectly sane, the orphan says.

We always follow the rules, says the Fresh Air child.

The bearded men speak to each other in their harsh foreign tongue. The men show them elaborate illustrations of the sort of behavior they are to avoid; in these illustrations, men are raping animals, lascivious children are having orgies, murderers grin at the erotic flowing of blood, women sport perms, boys deck themselves out in outlandish styles, and children of both sexes listen to radios.

We hope we will not have to confine you in the barn, the bearded men say.

The boys are set to work copying from the blackboard:

I live for those who love me.
Whose hearts are kind and true,
For heaven that smiles above me
And waits my spirit, too;
For human ties that bind me
For the task my God assigned me
For the bright hope left behind me,
And the good that I can do.

This room in the one-room schoolhouse is just big enough for a stage. The spotlight would fall on the two boys together, copying their words. To make the tedium bearable, the orphan spends this time telling the Fresh Air Child some of Beth's stories, changing just enough details to make the pathetic, unreal stories of abuse seem more plausible and entertaining. The Fresh Air child tells stories of his own, so that before long the orphan can't keep all the details straight, what is his story and what someone else's, what is real and what is made up. It's like a quilt or collage of missing paperboys, bondage scenes, mental institutions, drownings, dissected brains, and mysterious pregnancies.

The orphan has never been happier.

My sexual experiences have made me more cynical and worldly than you, he tells the Fresh Air child. I will teach you how to steal.

We have to escape from this farm, the orphan tells the Fresh Air child. Pack your bags.

The Fresh Air child says, Is this a farm, or a vast mental institution?

Is this what they call transitional housing?

We'll be musicians, says the orphan.

We'll be stars, says the Fresh Air child.

That night they slip down to the river with the electric guitar and into the boat and they float on downstream, far away from the farm. They travel for many nights and hear the barking of dogs on the shore and daytimes sleep in the boat back among the reeds. They leave their boat and wander on foot down streets where every family has two sons. The oldest son is always adopted, because the women think they are barren, or they think their men are full of faulty sperm. Either way, as soon as they adopt a boy, the problem corrects itself and they get pregnant. They wander past vacant lots and garbage dumps. Everything here is rusting or the color of rust. They wander through vast slums, and they wander through a pulsing, writhing concept of the world.

They receive rides from strangers who look familiar; they have taken leaves of absence. Somebody is muttering on the car radio, too quiet to be understood. It sounds like the future is trying to leak through. The practice of joy, one stranger says, involves the spontaneous rejection of one's belief or disbelief.

Joy should be embraced cynically, another stranger says. It is best to build up structures, unconsciously, such as some ridiculous "career", so that these structures can be ecstatically abandoned.

All joy is erotic, says a handsome stranger with a manly way. Joy involves the reversal of expected roles. For example, he says, and he whispers what he likes.

The landscape opens up into a different kind of desert. As if the earth has been stripped to its baked skull, as if the flimsy layers of skin and living tissue have been peeled back to reveal the bleached out substructure, the eye sockets, the mineral heart. It is electric. It is as if consciousness has eroded itself to expose the wasteland of eternity. Everywhere the orphan sees skulls gnashing their teeth. Hell's backbone and fluted walls. Aspen stands bleached and willowy like forests of ethereal bone dancing in the wind. Severe rock faces red as beating hearts or peaked mounds of grey. Skulls skulls skulls. Huge masses of cloud convoluted on top like the lobes of many brains cut off flat at the bottom, creating a plane in the sky parallel to the tops of eroded plateaus. Anasazi petroglyphs resemble Magnetic Resonance Images of the brain. Here at the bottom of a canyon a flash of pale green reeds dancing around a muddy ribbon. Against the muted colors of the landscape the river is insane: a rippling silver snake of electricity coursing through the dry rusty corroded landscape like a bolt of gleaming delirious metal in the brain.

What is the name of this river? the boy asks.

This is the same river that runs through your city, says the pedagogical stranger. It runs through your city and it runs through the farm and it runs through vast slums and deserts all the way to the ocean.

The river here is startling confirmation that every configuration belongs to him. Every face is his birthright. The face of his missing twin is a story about ecstatic submission and a revolutionary order. The face of the missing crazy girl is equally cunning and ineffective. The dust is in his hair. Compassion is his to choose not because it is the law, but because it is a deep and complicated pleasure which has convoluted the brain in a way only different from a tiger's. A tiger has stripes, he remembers. These stripes are madness. The orphan feels as if the lid of his head has been opened wide and that the catacombs of the sky *are* his mind: where thoughts are buried, where toxic chemicals go to die. The boys eat grapefruits throughout the day in an air-conditioned luxury car and at night the fixed stars and the satellites come out overhead. They build a fire and eat popcorn out of a foiled pie dish on a stick.

It seems here to the orphan that any action the living might take is of the ultimate consequence; he takes out his guitar. The human brain is crucial to the cosmos, the relationship between its two lobes and its potential new cauliflower growths. The immensity of time stripped bare in its purplish dance of colliding minerals and glacial damage, he says, only confirm the importance of the human faculty for music. Don't be so smug and pedantic, the Fresh Air child says.

How do families drive through this painted desert intact? he asks. The landscape should sever something. He gnashes his teeth at the sky. He calms down, eats a chocolate bar with some roasted marshmallow.

In the morning they find themselves in a valley of mushroom shaped rock formations. The top layer of stone erodes more slowly than the bottom layer, the stranger explains. Clouds like phantom frogs cross the sky and on the earth two male lizards with blue bellies engage in a pre-mating dance. They fight and chase each other to form a violent spinning circle unclear who is chasing who, until finally the smaller mounts the larger.

They drive on through scrubby high deserts with shreds of cloud so close he feels they might drive into them. Pale green shrubs with cerebral purple undertones. Cows once chewed on these shrubs. A waitress with a pinched face baked into an expression of vague disgust serves them pie.

The stranger leaves them in a city by the ocean. They walk around the docks and see all the pimps and whores and fishwives and sailors and petty thieves they had always known they would find here.

They gaze out over the water. All the orphan's intuitions in the desert were false, about the brain and the importance of "human" consciousness. He sees here that nothing matters, nothing at all.

He can't imagine what to do with the egg.

What should we do next? asks his lover.

He enters a tacky shop and buys a postcard. He writes: I am in the west now, and I am a rock and roll star. I have become rich and famous because of my catchy songs about sex and drugs and death and nihilism.

He affixes a 19-cent stamp and he mails the postcard to the farm.

Soon after, an epidemic breaks out. Almost the whole population of the City suffers from racking coughs and painful, bleeding sores.

Fun With Dick

Trebor Healey

I saw a youth in the wood today," she told Mortimer that evening, "brown-faced and rather handsome, but a scoundrel to look at. A gipsy lad, I suppose."

—From *The Music on the Hill* by Saki

Laughing boy, sweet glans wet, glistening silky semen, waterboarding.

It happened when I was young, and repeatedly.

Suckled, suckled, everybody suckle, suckle till the truth goes begging, begged, swallowed. They didn't wanna know.

So I lied about him.

Drowned.
A bush by the door.
Your bums all thrashed with rose thorns, sweetpie.

Only the plants are alive. I was born to a tribe of carcasses. Soymilk enemas, the doctor said, no other explanation.

And what does mother say when you bathe, the good Dr. Pinski implores.
Stay out of the roses.

I made salads of any kind of leaf, St. Joseph's aspirin, fruit loops and soy milk till I vomited and was waterboarded for my pains.

Laughing boy, you're my little pig on a spit he guffawed.

At the home, I can't have soymilk, they won't let me go outside. Florapathopsychosis they wrote on the paper. Poets, but dead ones.

They let me listen to Debussy and Sibelius though.

Aleister Crowley was a demon, you can't pick him.
Fuck their games. I choose Ronald Reagan to play instead and mutter through the game.. you seen one redwood, you seen 'em all, you seen one, all wood, one red, seen one, 'em, mmmmm, muah. Till they waterboarded me.

Rain especially. I'd go on one of those days. In the meantime I had a tennis racket I'd stolen from the rec. room. I made eyes in the webbing, a mouth: prunes and one limp asparagus. Till the thing smelled bad.

Laughed still. Stinking scoundrel. Pig corpse he barked, spitting on my glans, loogie slop sliding. Polar bears, waterboarded, having to swim to get Al Gore's attention. You seen one globe, seen one, muah. Fucking fur coat.

Wood never dies, it only rots. Soymilk enemas, the doctor said, no other explanation.

You seen one. Seen one? No, it's not possible. Waterboarding therapy.

One day I shit roses.

I wish he was a vampire but vampires don't laugh generally, they snicker, they have wit. I want to be a matador at least. I'm a red rose.

I couldn't get off my knees. That nurse, what a corpse. Let's get metal chairs! Keep it down, auntie. You seen one. Seen one? But we never thought.

Waterboarded and solitary. Steel, concrete, not even a window for the trees. The rain though. You seen one. You don't have to. It came for me.

Maybe a zombie, maybe I could be that much. You're my bitch he laughed, his glans bigger than an apple, a carameled apple only forever wet like rainforest glans. Eve of color in her little hut and Adam's got a bone through his nose. Boners and hicama and the rasp of my battered voice, creaking like an old wooden door.

Wrapped in white Chinese Silk. The last emperor. The only emperor. The once and future king. Arthur, Art, thou art healed, go and sin no more.

He's been alone! That corpse of a nurse. Jack Nicholson put up with nothing. You seen one. Nothing new under, and all is vanity. The Sun also rises and it sets and I wouldn't know about it. I'm a carcass, in a shallow grave. Nick Cave is the only one who knows I'm a horse, name of sorrow. Dwarves—not even.

Maybe it's puss? Diaper him she commanded. Get a mop.

Robert Frost is through with apple picking? More for me then.

He is the garden. Laughing, you stuck pig, ya—in cockney no less.

How'd you get so handsome—did you cheat?

Sounded like he was wearing heels in there. That's right, like heels, like high heels.

They fired her.

He's a danger to himself. Needs something to love the new animated corpse said.

One more waterboarding for good measure; vengeance more like.

I won't have it, not on my watch. Mad as a muffin. You seen one? Keep him out of the kitchen, there's no telling.

A plant. Something to love. She called him Charlie. I called her Magnolia on account of her reanimation. High honors. I asked for a cactus.

Denied. Not the waterboarding again, she cried. I like it. That was the end of that.

Hot cocoa and a TV, and you seen one transvestite... Are we having fun yet? Well are we? Full of love. Seen one. Fun. Fun, fun, fun, faun, laughing, no more waterboarding and bobbing for apples.

Stuck pig spinning like a kaleidoscope top. Orbiting obit.

Cactus, please, please.

One day they'll let me outside to bury me. What do they know. They seen one. Johnny Appleseed, the serpent and a brown girl with tits like tennis rackets, smelling awful. Well give her something sweet. She stuck it up Adam's behind.

He laughed.

A gipsy stole it—who else?

Stevie Nicks and the virgin birth.

Dim Star Descried

Sven Davisson

His name was Setna, though he went by Angel.

He seized my hand and Adam said, "...and hast received no harm in my glory."

The first time, he was wearing a black t-shirt, a fleur-de-lys disappearing at the edge of its left side, jeans worn a gentle variegated blue, and a white belt covered in a collage of skulls. Spiked hair, a goatee snaking the perimeter of his chin stained red in the moving lights.

At first a movement in my peripheral vision, I turned to look across the dance floor. Surrounded in a blazing coat of light. Outlined by the strobes, the tips of his hair a blond glory.

Fuck. I was made in that split-second. My breath stopped in a painful catching and Joe's story disappeared instantly.

Moments passed and I started breathing.

"Cade...?" Joe touched my arm. "Are you ok?" he asked as my eyes re-focused on him.

And behold our abode in your father transgressed the wet tongue. The line of David goes before thy majesty. He will give in paradise, but found wise they might be us? What have we to make entreaty to they that made themselves a side from nothing. Like what I felt in his confessions as we neared each others' dicks again, for approval; Angel winks, laughing, and the descendent of David turns as when she was ready. He expected respectively. We hold hands and five hundred come to worship Adam. "Be, which were revealed from each other mutually, as it were the other had reached Adam his last season." Finally, Setna went forth over the miles and was accursed from among them.

I turned to look back across the room. A new song had started and the floor had filled. "Fuck. Do you have a cigarette?" I could hear my heart beat its own disconnected rhythm smearing the music in my ears.

"I thought you quit?"

"I did. Do you have a smoke or not?" I had to grab onto something before I fell down the hole that had opened inside me.

"Sure... sure." He reached in the pocket of his hoodie and pulled out a pack of American Spirits. "Wanna go outside?"

"Yah, I could use the air." I finished off my whiskey—a large gulp that burned its way down.

"You all right?" Joe asked again as we exited into the alley behind the club. The emergency door locking behind us.

It didn't matter; Joe hadn't seen him. And besides he was off men this month.

He came in and stopped for a moment, ready for the battle, glowing in a surround of strobed light. He smothered me and left in the instance I noticed. He was one in a vicinity of stars. His wings actually screamed with fright, into the power of dripping cum and into the years of the shifted heavens. Like a fish caught glimmering in the moonlight he paused. In the slice of light I saw him down to his jockstrap and knew he was called Setna'el. His face was rallied against thee and his presence a crushing quietude of suffocating peace.

The blond stud's face, flush against the last decade, shall inherit the earth.

But all together reading the day's augurs—those he had strewn upon us... Shards of memory... only of his jacket and the jeans clutching his leg. I could not get his image, his hand, his base vanquished from my mind. The fading fragments were precious recollections to be known— treasures entombed somewhere in his phallus. Birds and beasts, they were all sitting on the fourth day. Later that night I would pump it furiously—images of light fleeing away before they could ultimately devour me.

Then the ram perceived the splendor of purpose; and his dick, showing hard, raced within him pinching his nipples. Drawing an extensive square, now to read their petition on skin, I went and spoke to the prophet: Hear me who art in bonds, O Marvelous Force, party... multiply me... Sleep-tossed and strange... working my tongue... hungering for an angel to redeem me.

I asked around, but no one else had noticed anyone new. Adam who bartended in the back on Friday nights couldn't remember serving anyone he hadn't served the same cheap draught to a thousand times before. Brian still wasn't speaking to him, but if anyone would know he would have. Why did I put up with useless drama, if he wasn't around when I needed him.

It became rumored that everyone had been in his pants. I was caught up in a frenzy of tension and possible truth; and never pared the whole. Period. I retained the superstition of sin against him. But dreamed of him in some pagan temple. And I was disappointed by his cock, stuffed it back in his jean. But when I awoke it spawned families of memories. I could get the fleeting image of his face, his body, the ways his clothes hung, the way they flattered his lines... I could not get his light out of my mind. The image of him possessed me like no other relationship I had ever had. Expending a decade on a lover was nothing akin to this passion five seconds invoked in me.

While middle-aged men fight, their troops numbering a dozen cascade over my nuts... their forefingers kill... the spider outnumbers an unlucky God. A third takes a passing shot at the children of men. And moves on into a zone of its own. He stated what residents might suppose; an ass stretched wider than the years. Definitely watching the laborious struggle to him and conversing slingers of stone. And him alone, he raised the shield, and seventy others joined in his march.

Angel had grommets in both ears and a bar across the back of his neck. When he smiled his childlike open-mouthed smile, one could see the glint of the silver ball sitting atop his tongue. In our first conversation, he tilted his head back slightly laughing, his mouth opened and I got instantly hard thinking about my tongue snaking around that bar intermingling in the soft warmth of bourbon.

He had angel wings tattooed on his back. They were carefully detailed in monochrome—the feathery tips tinged in flames of red and orange. They spread out across his shoulder blades and ran in soft swirls down his back. Not quite mirror-images, but one had to look hard. Between the two, at the top of his back, a cross was needled out in an intricate tribal conflagration.

He had twin stars on each forearm inked out in alternating red and black triangles. Trails swirled away from the one on his left like the tail of a comet. It's a falling star, he explained. Once I asked him why the right did not. "To remind me of what once was."

When, as the flood, the idea entered the earth.

From that first moment, when he seemed to bring a halo of ineffable light with him, I wanted him. Sure, that comes as no surprise. It was sexual, certainly, but way more than wanting to fuck him or be fucked by him. He possessed me. Somehow from that first, I knew that if he mounted me, it would mean more than his simple entering of my body. I would be consumed, like a scrap of paper in an inferno. The flame would first curl the edges and than I would explode self-immolated. How the fuck I sensed from moment one that having him would mean losing myself, I'll never know.

That night after walking Joe home, I couldn't think of anything but being consumed by fiery flames of emptiness.

Then life fucked back to my own cock, as I had been watching, I never met who our lord gave to him: There is nothing. I read their flock, one of them raised against him; a battle array, and God, time, our lord, said, "Come. His hand an estate passed from form, while all the others chalk, crumbling at the least ailment, a long succession of evictions." Both were swimmers to the fight. And they slammed into him, this guy, in even strokes, two eternal maledictions of purpose.

I scraped up some lube, mixing it with his white slippery load, and sprinkled it with them acquainted. You will—while another cries and they begin to be caused... they broke out again and heaven was drawn. His face, contorted with slamming, pushed into his light. I couldn't get laid out of respect for him, "There was this hot guy, let the other guy go forth and be brought out. And to devour them, until connected with a voice—still, different—his heart raced with angelic creation rose up from its course..." the day kills the spider unlucky again.

While the scraps of paper have shown the temple to be without a cross, it has become completely enwrapped in the bride that must be God's angelic creation... rising to see who it was, Angel continued the practice to establish my throne above all the days of reprimand in the Watchers' fall. The lord gave to them a blank sheet of justice and an open road.

This song is dedicated to Jello Biafra... cause I fucked his wife. It's called I Hate You.

The Exploited on the stereo and a rustle of the curtains awoke me. I'd left the window open so the bite of November might dampen the fire snaking across me like the flaming feathers of angel wings.

I pressed my head back into the pillow staring at the ceiling in frustration. *At least I got the ass, I shouldn't give a god damn... I'm so sad that you're so happy...* Undeterred the playlist shuffled on to Jinx Titanic. *Did you like your trip to the gutter... so sad... when your heart explodes cause I'm driving you crazy...*

"...Everybody here wants to fuck you..." Angel's voice was an almost inaudible breath in my ear as he preemptively echoed the lyrics of the next track.

Pillow magic alone can not brake the dreams... I pump him and breathe in his cologne, a transgressive scent of impiety completely formed in a slave's song, breaking his bondage as it extends itself to his natural length. My lubed cock sears electric wanting to enter him, I long for him to become captured with the unrighteousness of my eyes. He's walking out with one of my friends... seventy times ten his strength gives him considerable mastery of the angels. Their cocks hearken to the struggle... the American side unto me?? "This course the guys..." coming over as soon as he's off.... He stated that—splatted to the floor. Intelligent quadroon with many there...so gorgeous. He, the muscles of a thousand warriors, with torches putting to fire the holy spirit. Sheep must not look back as they bear great giants...Of the holy angels... former sheep again to trough...

I'd wake in the mornings Angel having left. I'd return in the evenings never knowing if he would be there. He made his way—his own quiet way—into me. I stopped worrying, for when he was there he was eternity.

The rhythm of our breathing moved together as we slept, as the sense of me moved to him when awake. *Like the preacher told you salvation won't be found among the sweaty writhing bodies so have an orgy underground...* We'd sit in candlelight smoking cigarettes and listening to the same Jinx Titanic CD. ... *Every demon's gonna know you.* He'd blow smoke rings toward me—their gray haze framing the curl of his smile. *You'll be shackled like a slave boy for all eternity...*

...if there's a hell we're burning burning burning...

This is side of dogs, foxes, and him a prince in the same. After saying this, his hand flies up his thigh. He surveyed the whole... this idea which entered execration shall be multiplied, and to reprimand my twitching dick. He strokes with a mighty notice that zips them, puts on to his left, then sin against birds, and the legs made more intense by conversed only with educated very ancient date—it made him a present of me and gave each that saw the inscription: "he I made contact with a voice came bidding...Voudoo John." He continued to find his peace; and they at first splattered black soot and lovingly smothered his will determined each line of wizards or after a laborious struggle in length.

Now the angels he couldn't afford and seventy times ten... and often of clear him... and there is known with a man... or ought to know idea which entered his with me a mortal happenstance victim of his fall...

"Even in immortality, life is too short for bad booze."

Angel stood at my counter, his bare back to me, a pair of black jeans low slung across his hips, the soft rise of his ass just peaking above the waist. He poured from a bottle of Laphroaig into two iced glasses. I looked to his left to an empty bottle of Jim Beam upended in the sink.

He turned and reached out with a glass. "An apple for the teacher?"

I sucked in air and the smoky smell of fired peat opened my nostrils. He'd splashed in just enough water to open up the flavor.

He raised his glass, "The blood of life." He moved as if in slow motion and drank with a wink. As he lowered his glass, his slight smile caught me by the throat. I couldn't breathe again. His beauty, his light, captivated me blinding obliterating all thought into searing white.

I took a sip of whiskey and tried to focus on the soft flavors. There was the smell of apples in the room. I focused on the narrow line of brown hairs trailing down beneath his navel disappearing beneath the top of his jeans.

He floated across the floor and put one arm behind me. Cold glass still in hand, I raised my arm across his back. I could feel the softness of the feathers as his tattoos wrote themselves into my flesh. I closed my eyes and breathed in apples.

Then my prick and foreskin extended halfway... ten thousand horsemen, and with their faces... covered. phalli... hearkened to the peculiar merit ... Angel ejected more fluid but continued to write out his petition, and the matter which I awakened... aid to recover the angels in this freak...people as a mountain... the giants

A spider seen in the matter which Setna'el... the third time our prayer in regard to... combing the hair...instead see the pair shalt have no peace: ceremonial, died some three... a child must not be the tribe; four distinguish battle... and the army this latter ram.

Then the peace; and they the whole of it.

He had a wide band of polished obsidian on his left index finger. At night while he slept the moon came through the skylight and caught it. He talked when he dreamed. He would tell fractured stories of Burgundy Street and the cottage on St. Ann. Some times I got the impression the threads of plot were lifted from another time. The dialogues were not of now. At others he would speak a broken French in an accent difficult to understand. As he dreamed the room would fill with a steam of seafood laced with the fire of red spices—of horses and cholera and the humid smell of damp stone. "And when he ate it was the third hour of the day..." he murmured one night as the moon glowed a dark harvest red.

Light ran music like antiquated jazz along his exposed skin as I watched him in the red moonlight. When I would finally sleep I'd dream of white skulls decorated in silver glitter. Their toothless smiles and empty eye sockets would move around me in a pattern alternating back into two-dimensions reminiscent of the belt he wore the first time I saw him. I remember a book I read once said you couldn't smell in dreams. But I know that's bullshit. Cigar smoke, red beans and a crawfish boil. A skull cradled in a ring of arum lilies and the corpus with blood dripping from the crude nail heads cradled in the arms of a young boy clad in a black cassock.

And in other nights he would talk in a quick archaic language like something lifted from a horror movie. I would imagine an old priest worrying his beads. Then, all of a sudden, he would begin a taunt, mid-sentence, the voice of a bowery queen drenched in sequins. Sometimes he would talk of himself in the third person—referring to himself as Michael. I knew, somehow, that he was always the subject of these fragments. In that concatenation of nights, stolen as fall approached the winter solstice, I pieced together fragments as if they were scraps of parchment hidden away for centuries.

Still other nights, he was just Angel. Well that was still just what everyone called him. We'd lie awake and he wanted to hear my stories. He wanted to know why I'd stopped singing with that hardcore band in college. What had caused me to be overtaken from one day forward with an unforgiving stage fright. An inexplicable reticence to be in a crowd... even if it was only singing in front of a tavern quarter-full of drunk punk kids. Why I stopped writing.

Why, if the meds stopped the visions, hadn't I stopped taking them.

"There was a time," he observed staring at the far wall, "when people were revered for having visions."

"Or killed."

"Well anything worth experiencing comes with no small degree of risk." He laughed at himself and took a long drag on his cigarette.

I looked into his eyes, while he slept, and saw of whom shall live and it made me so hot. A scent that drives and there is no more fluid but continued... As I was blood.

I lay half awake in the mornings, my hand cradling his semi-hard cock gently playing with his prince albert. I'd suck in the moment knowing that each morning was stolen on borrowed time. The titanium ring would go slick with pre-cum and he would turn his head to face me. His eyes opening out of sleep—each lit with a spark of white fire like magnesium burning in deep waters.

He rolled onto me lowering his head to my chest. Breathing fire from his mouth onto my nipple. His beard tickled my flesh. The unrelenting persistence of metal as he lashed his tongue against my skin.

Now the angels have out... And truth as he found, male nor female, and school is gradually dissipating the leader of which went forth... the heart melts or breaks... perpetually execrates...

"Don't think the Magi set out when he was born... That's just part of the Christmas bullshit. They had to have left at least two years before. The story says they followed a star. But did you ever think that it could have been an angel?"

He'd brought home a plastic crèche display drawn out in day-glo cartoon colors. The three kings looked like a 60's backing band done up

34

for Halloween as *I Dream of Genie*. Jesus looked like the Gerber baby. Mary and Joseph like Ken and Barbie at a renaissance fair.

"When the promise was not realized, where do you think that star went? Starfire is not extinguished in an instant. It takes millenniums beyond human reckoning to burn itself out."

I noticed he'd pierced his nipples. The open rings were formed of white metal that glowed in the low light.

Then Setna'el, called Angel, doing the stroking, surely a bit of cloth between the horse... *caballo*... I gasped and an exchange of names, rules... creoles...proud kind ... giant erection... powerful among them there is... upon an enemy. Once say to him, though, the heavenly Watchers.

...his eyes were inscribed with his name each a letter echoing as he kissed me. And thou shalt not battle God as the last drips of his spunk dropped onto my thigh—inasmuch as the guys were gone...

"Do you want to know where the other guys are now?"

I reached over and touched his face and it was suddenly like a child's... Finally tiring of his way, he became tender obedience... seventy times ten thousand to strike the sheep on the road.

When we got up in the morning not this marvelous which thou hast shown must have been. The young guy in the dogs caused to first devour them, until again it's back to full... but the sum of the first ram to drink the blood. His hands so generously reached out toward me to show me the south of his chest.

In the middle of the night I would reach out to his lingering warmth. He'd be standing at the window. His face a supranatural white from the street lights. His wings' feathers dancing red in the guttering candle light... He always turned sensing—I was awake—smile and return to bed.

I rolled him over... of the least multiplied...

anon seeks

Nicholas Alexander Hayes

Blank.

Search. Scroll.

Distance scalds.
Type. Post.

>Looking to give meat rose. Breed seed. Obey need. Blindfolded
>privacy, waiting.

Two beats.
Failure.

Type. Post.

>Looking for killing loads. Pump and dump; force and doubt. Raw
warmth.
>Charged and discreet.

Two beats.

Failure

Write. Release.

>Looking for killing meat. Force, pump and dump raw doubt. Breed
>privacy and obey. For now deep, deep insides charged with warmth.
>Waiting for discreet blindfolded need.

Responses:
Relief,
like sweet seed dumped,
like killing load released.

Answer: no limit set.
Now, attach: face, body.
       each pic, insides flaunted.
       each txt, pink surrendered.
       each wrd, desires told.

Time set; cold, blank space, a repository for impulses, singular moments,
is prepared.

>Awkwardness comes from the atmosphere, stumble. Hands on
shoulders,
>pressure left, pressure right, guide down. Flesh, limbs spiral.

Distinction cannot be established.

>One emerges: white flesh and soft muscle with black bristles. Back-lit

>face, shadow veil.

Warm quicksilver pools.

>One emerges: streaked and blushing rectum red, baby Buddha belly,
>lean face. Hand speed, craters picked into face reveal neither
>rest nor peace.

Small volley into suprasternal notch.

Fiery knot in gut seizes.
Nodule forms sends roots through windpipe.

>One lumbers holding heavy sow's purse. Back straddled, warmth
>spills.
>Magma dumped, slides from hole, between cheeks, ebbing around
>scrote.
>Succumbed to debts, world, reach for the sow's purse with left
>hand.

Mass moans. Chill; bodies veiled.

>Showered by sudden hailstorm. Beads glow pale blue.
>Teeth fracture.
>Spit enamel and blood over parched lips.

Strands drip over fingers to floor.

>The last, sallow flesh with green influences, remains. Rigid and

>brittle he stands. Above left hip a black tattoo reads, "Cleave."
>His kindness washes semen with piss.

>Skin scalds, pulls away from itself—
Curling webbed parchment from vellum.

Relief radiates, recedes, erodes leaving.

Five Views Of Mt. Fuji (After Hiroshige)

Will Aitken

1. Tokyo

A long reception room on the fifty-first floor of Tokyo City Hall. All that isn't glass is creamy marble. Waiters circulate silver salvers crowded with glasses of whiskey. "*Régarde*," Jeanne Moreau says to me as she opens her purse and takes out a small bottle with a glass stopper. "Vitriol for lying eyes." The room gives a sudden rightward lurch, then quivers like aspic. Whiskey glasses chime.

Toshiro Mifune rides to our rescue, his hair freshly carved from obsidian. "Earthquake," he rumbles, voice almost as low as Madame Moreau's. They touch glasses and bare their teeth. In their prime—in "Jules et Jim," in "The Seven Samurai"—they were immense and shimmering. In old age, at the Tokyo Film Festival at the end of the last century, they seem monumental in a different way, condensed and potent as fetishes.

Up on the dais a kimonoed woman wielding a big bamboo brush improvises a calligraphic poem across a stretch of rice paper as a string quartet plucks out a pizzicato rendition of "Strangers in the Night." With uncertain chopsticks I lift sushi morsels from a bed of unopened black and white mussel shells, neat and dense as Go markers.

Perhaps it is the fish and veg diet, or maybe the cup of cold sake bought from the hotel vending machine each night before I climb into my short, narrow bed, but after a few days in Tokyo, my skin glows pink, I start sleeping only two or three hours a night and feel energized, for the whole city delights me. And I, apparently, it. The closest I've come to living inside a movie musical. Shopgirls burst into giggles as I attempt to buy socks or an umbrella; anonymous hands snake out of the crush to grope me as I ride the subway at rush hour; uniformed schoolboys must have me at the center of their class photo as we leap together off a low temple wall, a golden cluster of out of focus monks smiling in the background.

Once again I find myself Japan-drunk and reeling, half a world away from the sobrieties of home.

2. Nagasaki

A dramatic beginning would be to say that I have come to Nagasaki in search of my father. Dramatic but untrue. I didn't know he had been here until long after I visited Nagasaki. Also, I would never search for my father for fear of finding him.

He was an officer in the US Navy, part of the American occupation force. He didn't talk about this time in his life much. I knew he had stayed at Frank Lloyd Wright's Imperial Hotel in Tokyo right after the end of the war and had been struck by the bathtubs, which were too short for a Westerner to stretch out in but probably just right for the puny Japanese. He didn't care much for the Japanese—"hissing yellow bastards" was one of the nicer things he said about them. Tokyo, he told me, had been more thoroughly devastated by conventional bombing than Nagasaki and Hiroshima had been by nuclear weapons. He was glad all the bombs—conventional and atomic—had been used because they shortened the war and saved American lives. I used to wonder whether his brutality had something to do with the war. But what to make of Tuesday's dream, in which my father's brutality led to the war?

He brought back with him from Japan a carved teak chest the size of a small coffee table (he said he had traded it for a carton of Chesterfields). At home we always called it the Chinese chest because, although it was Japanese, it was carved in the Chinese style. It came with a brass padlock with a grooved key. Inside were bundles of sepia Yen notes, handfuls of brown coins, wooden chopsticks in bamboo sheaths, handpainted paper fans in lacquer cases, diaphonous silk handkerchiefs, a couple of embroidered silk jackets and a pair of black silk pyjamas with orange piping and frogging, and dragons that rampaged up both sleeves. And stacks of beige photos of Japan, some featuring Japanese children with solemn faces, others showing my father grinning with his grinning fellow officers.

The photos didn't interest me much, but often when I was home alone I would retrieve the key from the cloisonné bowl on the mantelpiece, take out the various souvenirs and, laying them out on the carpet, examine them. They were like nothing else in our house or our town, and their beauty seemed apart from any other thing that I had been taught to view as beautiful. I would like to say that my exposure to these things led me to find out more about Japanese art and design, but I was a depressed and lazy child, and very little in my world then led on to anything else.

The last time I visited home, when I guessed it would be my last visit, once again when the house was empty I found the key and, shuffling through the photos that had not interested me before, selected a handful to bring back with me. In one, my father sits in a rickshaw, hands folded in his lap. He's in full dress uniform, including his black visored cap, while the Japanese man who pulls him also is in uniform, although his jacket and cap have been stripped of all insignia. In another photo, a young Japanese man, huddled in an overcoat too large for him, stands next to a hand-painted sign: "WELL COME!! THE FIRST BEERhALL in SASEBO WILL BE OPENED hERE BEFORE LONG FOR AMERICAN SERVICE MEN ONLY."

Sasebo is a naval base not far from Nagasaki. My father had been stationed there. On the back of the beer hall photo my father had scrawled the date, "14 March 46," along with, "All for honorable American Service Man."

3. Okinawa

Muki is a witch. I mean that in the nicest way. When she flies into the hotel lobby, copper-colored hair flaring out behind her, people stop dead, as though a spell has been cast. Across the gleaming terrazzo she's a gorgeous 21-year-old in a fur-trimmed denim jacket. When she shakes my hand she's a gorgeous 40-year-old. The way she carries herself suggests age is beside the point: she'll be a gorgeous 80-year-old too.

She drives with erratic surges of speed until she has passed everyone on the highway, but then she drifts, one hand on the steering wheel, foot no longer on the gas pedal, eyes just clearing the top of the steering wheel. This is an Okinawan highway at midnight, after the pair of us have consumed a shiny black earthenware bottle of *awamori*, a local favorite made from fermented and distilled Thai rice. It comes in 30-, 45- and 50-proof. You can guess which one Muki ordered. I think she told me she was a witch after we drank it. Maybe it was before. Tiny gnat-like cars, each holding half a dozen teenagers and a sound system bigger than the car, creep up on us, but the first headlight glimmer in her peripheral vision and Muki puts her foot to the floor again.

We're on our way to visit Muki's grandmother. When I suggest midnight is a late hour for visiting one's grandmother, Muki laughs and says, "It's all right—she's dead." I take this to be typically earthy Okinawan humor until Muki pulls up next to a roadside cemetery, with cinderblock tombs climbing up a stony mountainside.

Muki grabs a carrier bag from the back seat and I stagger after her up a gravel path. Near the top, a grove of trees sways beneath a swollen moon. Within the grove, Muki ducks into an open-fronted tomb. The back wall is mountain. A wide plank set into rock holds a vase full of wheat stalks, a box of kitchen matches, a coffee cup bristling incense sticks and a fat red candle. Muki lights the candle and then two sticks of incense, which she embeds in the melting wax. From her carrier bag she removes a tupperware bowl. "Egg flower soup," she explains, "Grandmother's favorite." Tinfoil flashes in the moonlight. "A nice porkchop too." She places on the altar a pale porcelain plate, which she arranges with biscuits. "Purple sweet potato cookies."

We sit in the clear moonlight and wait for Grandmother to come. "She was a witch too," Muki says. The wheat in the vase rustles.

4. Nagasaki

"Walking in the streets of Nagasaki," the travel poster reads, "you may meet a stranger." They're used to strangers here. Even during the centuries Japan was closed to the West, foreigners could come to Nagasaki, or at least to a small fan-shaped island in the harbor.

Everyone thinks of one thing when they think of Nagasaki, which seems unfair to this lovely city, spread out like an amphitheater across low hills and bounded by the sea and a wide crescent of green mountains. I go to the epicenter and try to think appropriate thoughts, but it is so hot—buzzing hot. Schoolchildren's chains of origami peace doves shift listlessly in the infernal breeze. I go to the museum and stare through glass at a skeletal hand fused with an amber beer bottle. Nagasaki wasn't meant for incineration, but the real target on August 9, 1945 was obscured by cloud, so the B-29 Superfortress flew here.

The heat drives me back to my room, which seems large for the rate I'm paying. After check-in, the manager showed me up personally, as though I was a visiting dignitary. I was still unpacking when the fruit basket and flowered bamboo arrangement arrived. Now I slip out of my sweaty clothes, shower and don the blue and white cotton dressing gown that all Japanese hotels, no matter how mean, provide. Pouring myself a toothglass of sake, I stretch out on the wide bed.

A knock at the door. The manager, a slightly stooped man in early middle age wearing a navy blue suit of managerial cut. "Good afternoon," he says and walks past me into the room. "Everything is satisfactory with your room?" I nod and smile to indicate my joy at the room. "And the view," he asks, "do you also like the view?" I join him at the window to admire the town and the choppy bay beyond. He glances at the fruit basket, the bamboo arrangement. "I see the gifts have arrived." I thank him profusely for them. From the mini-bar he removes two miniatures of Rémy-Martin. He smiles at me: "On the house." Pouring them out into glass tumblers, he hands one to me and sits down on the edge of my bed. I sit down in the desk chair, halfway across the room. Hands on his knees, he leans slightly forward. He looks as though he is ready to maintain this posture for as long as it takes. It's not only in the streets of Nagasaki that you may meet a stranger.

5. Fuji-san

Let's get the small hotel room jokes out of the way right at the top. Groucho Marx slouches out onto the vaudeville stage and announces, "My hotel room is so small the rats are stoop-shouldered." Incensed by this calumny, the hotel management demands an apology. The next night, Groucho comes out on stage, cocks his cigar. "I want to apologize for what I said last night. The rats in my room are not stoop-shouldered."

My first junket to Japan, I'm low on the pecking order of invited journalists. Judging from my hotel room, I'm in the basement. Welcome to the Akasaka Sakura room-in-a-cup. Add water, guest and stir. Standing room center, I can touch all four walls without straining. And yet, somehow, it is not claustrophobic. More like living at the heart of a finely calibrated machine. Everything I need is built in, from the radio alarm clock to the flashlight for finding one's way out of the rubble in case of earthquake, from mini color TV to the two copies of *The Teachings of Buddha,* one in Japanese, the other in English, tucked into a shallow compartment in the center drawer of the desk under the single window that has been rendered translucent for my privacy. A room with no view, then, but by way of compensation, the mini-bar tucked in under the desk contains three kinds of sake, four marks of whiskey, a split of champagne, seaweed nibblies and, inexplicably, a small glassine packet holding two SuperFine Mermaid condoms. I didn't know mermaids needed condoms.

The phone rings. My friend Jer, from Boston, who strings for the Los Angeles *Times.* He wants me to come see his room, up on the eighteenth floor (I'm on the fourth, the long ill-lit corridor just makes it feel like the basement). When the elevator stops at the sixth floor, a wedding party crowds in with me. The bride, in traditional kimono and heavy black wig, wears blue contact lenses. Her groom, immaculate in morning coat, is half her size.

Jer's room is so enormous it has a double door, as well as a window wall that runs its entire, protracted length. All is sharp, clean angles and sleek surfaces. The wet bar, larger than my entire bathroom, is fitted out with Lucite accoutrements—corkscrew, ice bucket, drinks tray, napkin dispenser. The white marble bathroom is blocky and awesome as an Aztec sacrificial site. "Pretty nice hotel," Jer says as he opens two bottles of Asahi. We stand looking out the window wall at the greyness of moonsoon season Tokyo. The clouds part and sunlight, which I have not yet seen in Japan, gushes into Jer's room until the white walls and furniture shine like a salt lick.

Jer's nose is up against the glass. "They said I'd be able to see it if the weather cleared. Wait! Is that it? No, over there, beyond that cluster of silver highrises."

I squint into the dazzling light and think I see—I may have seen—it, far in the distance, neatly poured as a pile of sugar. But then the clouds huddle together again and there are only the endlessly receding grey boroughs of Tokyo. A city sewn from felt. Wet felt.

Stall Three:
Meditation, Despair and Solitude

Stephen Boyer

Four large empty desks barricade the door to the restroom on the silent third floor, the literature section, a voiceless maze, undeterred I move through nude space, occasionally bumping into ideas bulging from books, enter restroom. Wash hands.

Stall two is occupied, why is stall two occupied? It's rarely occupied. Usually I open up to anus god naked on stall two unbedazzled

white and ordinary and full of shit... My ass is the altar...

Instead I take stall three. Some of my contemporaries enjoy the luxury of weeping and singing to their fictional god untroubled so why must I endure this unidentified neighbor's noxious odor as I

delight in my weeping singing

? I shouldn't have eaten the

pizza, it's making this unbearable and my heart beat rapidly.

Rich kids content themselves with junk food.

This isn't a sublime shit; it's reddish, vile, full of carbs.

I find the sublime when a shit is so large my entire being is forced to feel its passage from my body or when brownish green gushes quick, out, floats across or when the smell is strong enough to call to Lord Byron—popular applause—'But I neither love ye, nor fear ye; and though I buy with ye and sell with ye, I will neither eat with ye, drink with ye, nor pray with ye.'

I am alive.

Community college offers nothing so community college students raid ethnic cheap dives and learn there are a variety of foods. I should have stayed in community college. Learning for the sake of learning is what I found; now I'm learning to be a snobby android warring for scholarship funding. USF gives students cheap corporate half ass attempts at taste and nutrition, this must be part of the dumbing down of American youth a media controlled and reason for my chunky carb shit.

Stall two squeaks so I fart back.

My body wants an enema but I'd have to venture out of the stall to fill a plastic tube with water; one must exploit. I learned

exploitation equals cleansing

from a business student. Pants at my knees, filling plastic with water, reaching for paper towels, surely a priest would enter. Maybe then I'll get a scholarship? Instead I try not to think about time

focusing on the present I see grey tile, beige walls, hear the neighbors shifting body, beige ceiling, white bright light above so I can't pretend this sterile environment offers anything more than banality desolation silence

Last night electro music, dancing, alley sex, body as water and drugs, neon lights;

my present life is shit. On the toilet I suffer no anxiety.

I spend ninety percent of my typical day in horror...

did I shit myself? Stall two flushes.

Shitting myself never happens; nevertheless the image constantly haunts me. One day I will buy Depends® and never worry again.

Knowing

I can bridge my daily life with my toilet life

will unravel me into complete freedom. Ah, the ass, the temple... its manifestations its testament of power... the sphincter gateway to my heart.

I wipe. My external layer cleansed, I wrap paper around index finger and gently insert, rub my gateway.

When I go home I will masturbate till spinning disco balls again and again radiate, my mind racing into clear full sound.

I stick finger repeatedly into

Batailles' fetish gleaming as

I stare into a collection of his poetry spread, his dripping wordy cum covers the bathroom floor, each time I reach deeper, take it all in my eyes, mouth and nose. Brain wanders, eyes peek through space beneath door black shoes exit stall two. His smell reaches out from whirling water swooshes through my ear canal. Drop tissue into toilet. Unwind more, again I caress my anal, imagine

his face, my whore, reaching hands over desiring skin, the nothingness inherent in all eyes in his staring into bare space, his despondency, hairy balls full of cum busting on my face, life as an event you are high with tingly orifices, licking his asshole stretching open and its inevitable closure as he washes his hands, he sees the act of defecation as dirty so he cleanses himself from deliverance, makes his way through the hushed empty library full of unread books;

a sanctuary for meditation, despair and solitude; and laughter and snickers and snorts nervously erotically humanly

Yolk

Tom Cardamone

Masa woke naked, floating in an egg. He had not shrunk, rather the egg was large, big enough to contain him, allowing him to stretch and drift, content and warm. Too sudden a movement, however, and he would brush up against the shell. Not that it was a very large egg. Still it was more comfortable than confining. Immediately he sensed that he was inside an egg because he was embracing a large, wholesome yolk, the way your typical sleeper might hug a favorite pillow. The yolk was centrifugal, Masa happy to hold on, feet out, the surrounding current of viscous albumen flossed his toes, cupping his muscular calves. The yolk glowed a soft yellow; an inviting amber. The enveloping egg-white swirled slowly and Masa felt as if the silk of the albumen were the milky rings of a planet; that he clung to a fragile world.

He let go of the yolk and slowly drifted. He painted the interior wall of the shell with his fingers; it seemed firm, with a rough consistency. And hard. This barrier would not be easily broken.

The glow of the yolk pulled him back. Knees up, he brought his fingers around the yolk to more fully embrace the mass. Warm egg-white knuckled his anus, the sensation spurred his erection. His bobbing cock lightly punctured the yolk; he felt electrified. He could see the shadowy curvature of his penis submerged in fluid gold—he'd always delighted in the uniquely sharp tip of his cock—the way the tight foreskin bunched rather than retreated, giving a decidedly pointed, sword-like appearance to his already angular prick. The hair on his forearms wavered in the egg-white, looking to him like a giddy paramecium.

He dug his fingers into the yolk and it roiled. He pushed his forearms in deeper, up to his elbows. Within the confines of the shell a milky hurricane now unhurriedly churned. Phlegmatic shards spun off the central mass; a long tendril forced his lips apart to splice through the tiny gaps of his clenched, crooked teeth. The smear of egg-white that had lightly adhered to his eyes rippled, distorting his vision. This pressure intensified; he shut his eyes. Overwhelming darkness descended as the yolk, his center of gravity, dispersed; private universe in turmoil, his whole body clenched. Balled like an infant he ascended until, cupped by the cusp of the egg, he felt it tip and fall.

Masa woke in the bed of a stranger. The mattress was vast, a great plain. Bedposts rose like massive, black twisting tree trunks, their dark canopies joined far above. The high, minuscule points where the leaves interlaced shone the pinprick likeness of distant stars. Paisley sheets bunched and gathered, rolled like hills and valleys.

And there were tigers.

Black tiger, white tiger. Far off, eyeless beasts, giant cats that relied solely on a powerful sense of smell, roamed. Their joint roars crashed against the sheets. Masa cowered. He wore a tight tuxedo, high on his wrists and ankles.

A small flat fish clung to the ground like a foot print. It was a spiny flounder with poorly matched eyes fearfully searching the dry sky. Soon Masa noticed more of the fish sprinkled about; they were numerous, forming the paisley pattern that comprised the sheeted ground. These configurations were punctuated by weird, equally spiny shells, ancient mollusks and empty horns powdered with sand, their pink whorls pulsated with thirst. They were interspersed with black sand dollars. Shiny ebony discs caught the false starlight and flashed it back toward Masa.

The man with antlers stood high on a hill of fabric.

The man with antlers circled Masa while still keeping his distance. Masa kept an eye on him while peeling off the tuxedo. Naked, he felt free and buoyant, the giant mattress a sudden moonscape, littered with a school of fish beached in a teardrop mold. The folds of the sheets formed dry streambeds. Masa, arms out-stretched, ran down one such lane, care-free and smiling, the moon-breeze brushing his cheeks.

As he turned a bend in the stream he surprised the man with antlers.

The man with antlers stood still, wary but curious, sniffing in Masa's direction with a wet, black nose. Tufts of brown, dirty hair sprouted from his shoulders. Otherwise he was nude, save a thick pelt which clung to his pelvis like moss. His skin was startlingly white. They circled each other. Masa noticed that the knuckles of the antlered man were red and cracked, as if he had recently been in a fight. They froze as twin tigers roared nearby. The man with antlers extended his hand. Masa took it and they sprinted down the dry streambed, away from the hungry howl of big cats.

They paused beside a bramble of driftwood bleached ghostly gray by inconsistent moonlight. They disentangled sweaty palms. Face to face, he examined his new friend's asymmetrical antlers. They rose from his temple like sturdy branches. Both were a gray ivory, darkened by multiple fissures. Each clutch possessed a different number of blunt points. Possibly some were broken off in forgotten duels. The man with antlers grinned. Masa smiled, too. Leaning in for a kiss he was surprised by the coldness-wetness of the man with antlers flat coal-button nose.

On his knees, Masa rested the palms of his hands on the boney ridges of the antlered man's feet. He delighted in the minute shifting of the man's toes, keeping time with the administrations of his tongue.

A nearby flounder, stapled to the ground by two corn-colored teeth, watched with wide, distraught eyes.

Masa woke up underground. Moist clumps of dirt hung from roots, dripping from a low yet unseen roof. It was hot in the cave. Fearful, Masa rushed forward, worried he would become mired in the soft dirt if he stood still, and that the loose dirt above would come crashing down. It was dark. He hit an earthen wall and pushed. It gave way.

Masa stumbled out, a slight avalanche spreading at his feet onto a grimy subway platform. This subway stop was still under construction. Lanterns hung from the low, still-earthen ceiling. Wheelbarrows of raw concrete were parked beside sharp pickaxes. The rumble of distant trains vibrated across the newly-tiled landing. A huddle of workers blocked the only exit of shiny metallic turnstiles, roped-off with yellow police tape.

The workers turned toward Masa. Big men slick with sweat, granules of dirt clung to their oiled bodies, massive shoulders pushing their torsos forward. Their small, mammalian faces were obscured by miner's helmets, each with a dim, cyclopean lamp. Large buckteeth buttoned lower lips. The Beaverhead closest to Masa approached. He had shovels for hands. His flattened fingers were fused together; his long, protruding thumbs wiggled constantly, as if proudly proving their independence. Masa stepped back. A train approached. Its horn sounded loudly. Masa peered down the tunnel. The train was actually a massive white worm, penile, eyeless and subterranean, inching forward on the force of its ribbed form. Masa sensed that the thing was endless. A huge lamp shone harshly out of its central drooling slit onto the freshly laid tracks. It struggled against the walls of the tunnel. Clumps of dirt fell from the ceiling. Beams buckled. The approaching Beaverhead plunged a shovel hand into Masa's chest. Masa reeled and stumbled back. More dirt fell. Masa turned, crying out in pain. He felt deeply stung. The Beaverhead had tried to pry loose his soul. The train-worm wailed as the tunnel collapsed in an endless roar of dirt. Masa dove toward the closing hole from which he had emerged.

He woke up inside Guillermo. Guillermo was his first lover at college. Neither of them spoke English well, nor did they understand a word of each other's native tongues. But they had smiled at one another on the soccer field, exchanged furtive glances in the dormitory showers. Now Masa was inside Guillermo, but not in the sense of their previous, rhythmic fusion. He was fully inside Guillermo, he wore his skin, filled his body with his own. Raising his hand he saw Guillermo's strong, stubby fingers, the bitten nails, the wide, honest palms. Masa sat up.

He was in Guillermo's bed, back at college in his lover's dorm. Sheets bunched at his feet. His boxers were twisted low on his waist, cracking the fly open, a thatch of Guillermo's bristly, ebony pubic hair rushed forth. Masa ran his fingers over his lover's chest, lingering at the polished copper pennies of his oval nipples. He felt Guillermo's cock stir and push against his boxers. Blood raced through the protruding veins of his forearms. His heart beat within Guillermo's heart, this double-engine fueled Guillermo's engorged cock. It rose steadily, meeting sweaty palm. He pressed the blunt fingertips of his other hand to his lover's dry, cracked lips. Their salty taste churned memories of surreptitious meetings after class. Thanksgiving, vacant hallways, their only uninterrupted weekend together. The first time either of them had seen snow. Masa's own erection filled Guillermo's like liquid metal. A shifting pink necklace of foreskin tightened as one erection threatened to push through the other. His lover's body unraveled as orgasm rose. Guillermo's chest split into ribbons and fell away as the first rivulet of semen pearled. Masa's thin, neat fingers scissored through his lovers hands. He felt his own true tongue wipe Guillermo's perfect, strong teeth.

His buttocks involuntarily tightened.

One leg jerked.

Cream startled his boxers with a milky pattern like the thick white folds of wax paper.

Masa woke up.

The Magus Club

Craig Laurance Gidney

Lice were everywhere on the Corpse, but they are particularly populous on the Underside, between the Scrotum and the Anus. With chittering mandibles, they feast on dead flesh, tearing white flakes with their serrated jaws. The pilgrim watches an abundance of legs and translucent taupe bodies as they graze. It is beautiful, the patterns of lace and saliva they make of the scales of skin. He could watch them forever, as they slowly chew the expanse to nothingness. But he can't ignore the Call in his body. It plays over the cobweb network of his nerves, a tintinnabulation that won't end and drives him on and on.

He felt the Call as soon as he arrived on the Corpse; everyone here obeys some epic urge. His memory, his name all vanished, to be replaced by the hideous electric itching Call that drove him across the Corpse. Over the Nipples, and the vast expanse of the Belly.

Strange cities sprouted on the rotting ground of the Corpse. Structures of bone and gristle, cemented by blood and bile, where tame lice hooked up to rickshaws patrolled narrow streets. These cities, lit by energy powered from the dying brain waves and rigor mortis, were dangerous places. They were glorified slums for criminals, ruled by cults and tyrants. Brothels full of succubae and catamites festered like infections in their alleys. The pilgrim avoided them.

The Call drove him through areas fouled by clouds of decay; he would wrap rags around his mouth as traveled through corrosive yellow mists. It drove him around craters filled with old brown-red blood. The Corpse had been tattooed; the tattoos slithered beneath the dermis, animated symbols.

He spent a month in the scabrous caves of the Nose, nesting among its grey hairs, trying to reconstruct his past, to no avail. A syllable of his name would dance on his tongue, just beyond reach. A face would hover in memory, only to fade just as quickly. Was he in some kind of hell? After a while, he grew to accept his amnesia. It had its benefits, and he was soon to discover that all who lived on the Corpse had lost their names and identities.

He traveled over the dome of the Head, where follicle-trees fell and crashed every moment. There were fewer pilgrims up here. Most of them were hermits, driven mad by their own Calls. It was in the Eye that he first heard of the Magus Club. It was rumored that sorcerers could remove the Call from people. Maybe they could restore his name.

The club lies just beyond the herd of lice. He is prepared, having encountered the wild monsters in the Pubes. During the journey on the Buttocks, he collected dried pustules, warts and the meaty strands of hemorrhoids. He draws them out from his briefcase, waving the sores in front of him. Meat and dust. Transparent bodies pause, scent the air and eyes that jewel the ends of antennae flicker. He tosses a wart in the air, and the herd of lice disperses, heading toward the treat. The pilgrim throws another one, and more lice leave in its direction.

Just as he is tossing the last of the encrustations, a fellow pilgrim bursts from behind a copse of pubic hair and takes advantage of the diversion. The pilgrim is annoyed, until he sees the man is followed by a louse not distracted by the bait. It trundles gracelessly, still quicker than its prey, and overtakes it. Anguished cries, the snap of bone and tendon: they are hard to ignore as he slips past the scene. The stench of voided bowels and exposed viscera raises vomit in his gorge.

The ground shakes. Another volcanic fart burbles from the Anus. The sphincter quivers, and a staircase of stench climbs the air around him. The pilgrim skirts the lips of the Anus gingerly; it is encrusted with old excrement, so he presses a rag to his nose again.

Catching his breath, the pilgrim looks around, taking in the architecture. It wavers in the perpetual twilight and never settles on a single style. The bewitched building materials are stone, wood, mortar, thatch, stucco, iron, brick at any given time. It's as if the building can't make up its mind and erases and redraws itself. The pilgrim gets dizzy focusing on the myriad nascent forms that stretch and curl before him. Gothic cathedrals collapse into suburban compounds which erect in turn rusting warehouses. Hybrid forms are created: Indian temples with automatic doors; medieval monasteries sprouting the metallic fungus of satellite dishes; castles made of adobe.

Voices drift on the breeze, soft and subsonic and full of sibilance. Snatches of song, gasps of ecstasy or agony, a run of laughter all tickle his ears. The pilgrim feels the very ground beneath his feet—that shifts from dirt to flagstones to cobbles—vibrate with footsteps and their echoes. The sounds add themselves to the Call that reverberates through his brain. A clatter of pipes. A soothing female voice that bleeds into a scream. Waves that crash and hiss. Glass that vibrates then shatters. The buttery sound of a horn, the lonely cry of a loon. All fill his ears.

The pilgrim is assaulted by all sorts of smells—the antiseptic sting of industrial chemicals, rotting food, gas, overripe fruit and flowers. Salt spray, honeysuckle, the freshness of snow, motherly vanilla, the humid smell of shit, the taste of ash in the air...The walls, whatever material state they are currently in, sweat the odors out.

The pilgrim stands still for a moment, adjusting himself to the swirling chaos that surrounds him, the sensory and synethestic overload. Then he goes forward on his quest.

The door to the Magus Club is wooden, warped by time and darkened by soot and grime. A face, pocked and nude, is carved in the wood of the door. When the pilgrim approaches, the closed eyes splinter open, and a green lambency oozes forth.

—*Enter me*, the wooden face croaks in a resinous voice. And it *flows* down the mottled, wooden surface of the door until it is level with the pilgrim's crotch. The lips part, revealing a red, pulsating gullet. It is obvious what key he must use to enter the club. The pilgrim unbuttons his trousers and places his flaccid member down the wooden throat. The interior is smooth. The wooden lips constrict around his cock, tightening around the base. There is a rumble as the sucking mechanism commences. The pilgrim feels the velvet slipperiness and there's a flash of memory:

a face of flesh with a cleft chin slowly licking his body down to his cock, ingesting it, the strains of Nina Simone's contralto in the background, a ceiling stained with the brown islands of watermarks—

and the memory slips away.

The vibrations stop after a moment, and gears and cogs shift as door swings open inward. The pilgrim adjusts his fly, and steps in the hallway.

The floor of the hallway is tiled in mirror, reflecting the black emptiness of the ceiling above. The walls are bone-white and luminous and cast a triptych of shadows that distort the pilgrim's every step. A few steps down the corridor and he hears the door close behind him with a thud. The walls are as soft as flesh, and as pliant. They hold the memory of his fingerprints for a moment before smoothing out. And a flash of memory:

other flesh that held the memory of his fingerprints, a green glass ashtray overflowing with butts, bodies tangled in each other and sheets with paisley designs—

The Call is louder here than it ever was. It is now a silver needlethin scream that leads him down the hallways of gauze and flesh. Perhaps he will end up mad after all. The Corpse is rotting; why wouldn't it rot the minds of those who lived on its surface? He glances down in the mirror-floor, and sees his own face. The hollow eyes, the gaunt cheeks, and the sallow undertone to his dark skin: he barely recognizes himself. He is a walking corpse on the Corpse. Did death do this to him, or the Call?

The hallways of the Magus Club twist and turn like vines. The passages veer off to the left and to the right, with no logic. Rooms grow like tumors. Honeycombed through the living walls, most of them are dark and empty. But every now and then, the pilgrim will see an occupied cell, protected by a thin membrane, like a transparent eyelid.

In one cell, a photographer develops pictures endlessly. The pilgrim pauses to watch him work in his red-lit darkroom. Images of flowers and Negro genitalia emerge from chemical baths. The photographer obsessively places them on the ovoid surface of the walls, where they are absorbed. "The flowers of negritude," whispers the pilgrim.

In another cell a black writer with the white hair of Santa Claus writes on his cell's wall. The words are backwards, dyslexic, and they vanish as each sentence is completed, slowly turning in a vista that shows a decaying industrial city lit by two moons.

The Call draws him on, past other rooms and scenes.

A group of men, gaunt and wasted, form a circle jerk and their mingled seed creates a pearl that glows. *Pearl-seed*, the pilgrim thinks.

Fathers of pearl.

A philosopher, bald and bespectacled, reads revolutionary texts while being whipped by a boy the color of coffee with cream.

He knocks at each door, begging for entrance. The inhabitants ignore him, concentrating on their own madnesses.

The Call is unbearable now. It rings and reverberates through his body, rattling bone and brain. He turns a corner, and sees *it* in one of the honeycomb pods.

The Call.

The Call is a man made of sound. Flesh that sings, muscles that pulse, blood cells that are notes. A soundwave in human form. And another flash of memory:

bending over synthesizer modules and flickering computer screens and guitars, creating hymns to the chthonic soul within—

He was a musician. This much is clear. He took sound and shaped it. Anything and everything was his palette: the sound of insects, the voices of scholars were woven within his abstract compositions, giving life to dreams.

The shape of the man of sound is his own. It wears (or *sings*) his face. His name is hidden in the notes.

The pilgrim approaches the membrane that separates him from the thing he seeks. The membrane does not give. The pilgrim withdraws a knife from his briefcase, and pierces the stuff. It parts, and he catches a scent of the marvelous music within. The gash immediately fills, becomes whole and impenetrable and silence descends. It is a waterfall that hardens to diamond. The pilgrim beats against the no longer flexible membrane, until his palms are bloodied. His soul sits in the honeycomb cell, blissfully unaware of the tumult. The soul shimmers with decibels. The Call is louder now than it's ever been. The frequency shatters his density, separating the very cells of his body. His ears and nose begin to bleed.

The pilgrim slides down the glass doorway, leaving a smear of blood that is absorbed by the sheet of diamond, tinting it cruel pink. It is useless, his whole life or afterlife. *Curse it all. This horrible Corpse.* If he could, he would destroy it all. Weeping, on the floor of mirrors, he says a Name.

In a sound like crashing glass and falling water, the membrane falls apart. The awful Call that's followed him for ages in the dead lands ceases its ringing. The pilgrim stands and smiles, dripping blood, and steps into the cell. The cell closes again, leaving two occupants in the cool interior. The man of sound rises and approaches the man of flesh.

Face to face, they kiss. Lips locked, they devour each other, saliva and sound, until they permeate each other. Flesh and wave absorb one another.

Hybrid and hyphenate: they are a new creature, imbued with a new quest. It is the goal of all of the prisoners of the Magus Club:

What spell will resurrect the Corpse?

Submergences

Jeffery Beam

This one for Richard Fitzpatrick. Rest peacefully.

꙳

A writer starts out to describe a kingdom of castles and horses, but ends tracing the lines of his own face. —Jorge Luis Borges

If a lion could talk, we could not understand him. —Ludwig Wittgenstein

Natural things exist only a little; reality lies only in dreams. —Charles Baudelaire

I become a transparent eyeball; I am nothing; I see all. —Ralph Waldo Emerson

I am obscure as feeling is. —Pierre Reverdy

The altar...is anywhere you kneel. —Camille Paglia

Submergences

၄၅

To enter. The heart must shatter.

၄၅

It all began empty snow-white black velvet: an assault on the dark edges. Crickets howled at the house. The house lay secret, wanton. A gross bile echoed in the rooms. Rooms of toys rooms of gingham rooms plastered with a child singing in the night his arms flung out the window into a southern inflated summer of crepe myrtle and violets. Wine plum cerise starlight flickered on my tiny feet shuffling to the window. A tiny narrow garden a smoky garden a frightened and frightening garden shivering in its horrible aspect of sweet ambassadors hidden among flowers. And a voice whispered to me in the darkness, to the child of age the child of woe whistling in the mirror the darkeyed child the secret child the child alone the childman leaning out the window:

Let your hair barely bronzed naked tattooed in scarlet the marks where the act lives in joy, dies with better hope.

I knew, then, the being inside this ribbon of flesh. I knew the ribbon stroking the darkness.

၄၅

Rims of scarlet. Gold. Olive leaves. Rims of thickness descending on arcs of ruby. *Mica. Fluorspar. Tourmaline.* Silver white purple loose blackness. The mirage.

❦

I am a child, watching words form in my mouth which then fall clumsily to the floor—remarkable, magical communion with godliness. I am responsible towards these words. Taking us somewhere we have not been. Defining the world, the known.

❦

Beautiful beautiful life with what has been and has not been me asking to become part of something it has not seen and seeing it part of me within it part asking to understand and understanding again its silverness its part which shines and the dull the whole beneath the inside and lightning lightning no not fleece but unbearable seeing which knows O knows so seeing inside beautiful life beautiful life asking of nothing asking.

❦

The thing which is beauty. Is itself. Broken. Light under a cornice. In a wayward room. Unvisited.

❦

Here are the young. They beat the white hairs on our chests until we cry to love them. Ravenously, I pluck hairs stuttering at the fall of some most holy penitents.

꙰

Always water. Always loose weeping because we dare not blame ourselves.

꙰

You will say you remember me on that last day when frozen we stutter through ice. You will say motion is between us, that years of speaking to and for each other has its boundaries, has a word or meaning or symbol discernible in the future beyond our pain or invisible hatred of departure and that we are its captive. But I have the odor of your lips next to my eyes. I cast off the weight of poison the dart your odor spins into my heart. The ice forces my hands into an arch, a yogic tempo of pleasure shooting through them. I forget odors and figures I forget the seething power of hatred the seething power of blueblack wounds and the rush of blood to the temples. Our journeys, perilous. My vapors mix with the infinite.

꙰

Outside the moon eats at white shadows
with its mirror
Night's green glare
simmers in the woods
The sleepers gone

Wild lilies stare at the stars
Three in the morning

the fire trains lions in a circle of weeds
The lions hearts of red hawks without eyes

The lilies weightless
dragging their carcasses behind them

The sleepers rustle in coat sleeves

Now the moon shudders
at its face in the mirror
nudging the fire
As lions swoop among the pines
sleepers sweep the ashes
mocking its restlessness

And the Shadow enters me. Enters the snapdragon path in the center of my chest, the bronze being murmuring in my stomach, captivated by release, captivated by the body of pain. I remember now the vast sun unpeels its skin each winter—a lizard. The golden chiefs give feathers of blue to hide their magic in ... women of citrus gather blossoms the moon gives them soaking the petals for oils. The sleek triumph of a man's body insistent all-owning transparent tiger-lilies lasting only an hour in the jar. Married in water divorced by it shimmering evaporate, my skin moults in the jar, leaving a residue of fragrance and blood, residue of light boiling in the bowl. Death strides through my belly, awakening the mum-odor of silence, a vast unbreakable silence pure as granite thick as noon snow. As I turn, a face lifts its fisheyes from the snow. Quietly the white settles on my shoulder. Alone with the moon, my ointments bleed into the streets, leaning forever against the dragonwings of the sun.

❧

The heart palpitates under the windows. Pane after pane. Reflecting bubbles in the glass. In clear domes, the way light cowers in the corners. Waiting to be discovered.

❧

We brood heat in a glacier. The glacier descends in perfect rhythm as I deny its closeness. But the cold belt soothes, chipping away at the green carousel: my memory of the future. I look graciously forward, aware that you have touched me. The tiny cilia of doubt sipping at ice: fear of the unknowable blank margins of space where I forfeit control to the inner world. I give in. The glacier swelters, crushing my imagined freedom. The inner voice. The unknown.

❧

A white line on a wharf. Decade after decade of facing the firing. Dull gulls, mink cups from which we drink words. Reckless and starving, leaving exhilaration behind with monotony. Afraid to believe.

❧

We hurtle toward oblivion. Holding ourselves back but crazy with the desire to unite with it. What is the unknown?

Against your hand
my body twists a flower
struggling to blossom
Pollen sweating through the stamens

We clamor   now   at the center
of the sun
My waist rising out of a pit
churning you wet

I gasp   bleed minerals
feeding the root
Its exotic urge
separating sweetflesh
from the spirit
while I rage
at transient intensity
flinging the hole of the body
into space

This fever I know
unlocks gold
A mystery stone
A potion
seen in dreams

Charting the course
we might take with love's body
my waist
held in your hands
Slipping wetness from vials
eroding the foundations of your heart

❦

Thrown weeds caught between my legs. Pollen devouring the naked man running over pebbles his earrings his ears black with unspoken words unheard themes. Insects eating at the semen's gore. I draw three circles round the lizard. His tongue a rock. Twists of the lizard's tail point towards the stars. I buckle into sleep.

❦

The lapse of time between the initial glance and the final expected moment of confrontation seems like ages. Time, when one is hesitant, when one cares deeply and awaits much, drags—a web of spidery silk, snagging every effort to move, to complete the journey from one room to the next. The rose grows thorns and buds. The vine gathers its mesh. The web: embracing a shiny ebb-quiet rowing towards love—mixed blossoms with fragrance impacted so strong I feel no guilt, no hesitancy to complete the collision. Interstices of the dream.

❦

The wind knows no one tonight
but we
The sleepers thick under
the stars
We have no arms nor legs
nor torsos
No ground
nor seed

We who have not the urge
have not the sense
We who have
shiver in quintessence

ᑫ丂

The kind murder of renunciation. A velvet bomb exploding hate's retina.
I learn to love, learning to hate. Hate rises out of the body, flagellating
the senses, penetrating layers of myself. Testing my strength. The quick
sleeve of guilt stifling efforts to move and be. Love releases guilt. Releases
hate. Trial by fire and the whistle.

ᑫ丂

Using the body as a tool to realize
itself
in all its infirmities
bloodpassing
through watery soap

Using the sweatboiled rim of skin
hung in an arc
on a band of light
Crazy light of fabulous fingers
in the core

ɞ

Where are your hands that have touched? Where the soul in your eyes? Hair down deep—fish in gull wings singing. You know the fairy tale. You, the hands that bleat in darkness. The root. Wild refreshing billow of hands. Pillow of hands. My pillow: a nail hammered in red parachutes of tourmaline. Your hands pigeons in my back. Arched holy saints of fishes. Hands in their blue suits of love fishing out whales humming in alabaster.

ɞ

I come before noon with wind anchoring my stomach. Wool banging shutterless against dawn and your hands. I am the black sparrow you knew. The cautious lover tucked under your brow. The beaten paradise. I cannot see, needing your hands trumpets of wine and smoke chattering my tongue. My waist. My infinity in your hands.

ɞ

If I dismantle the cragginess of lips—lamps without oil. If I lay both sides of a coin on the groin of words—a bitter green like a wild form. If I persuade the sickness to come out—morning will rise with the hooves of angels on the streets.

❧

Aphrodite bore me from the waves
neither son nor daughter I am
the mixed bloom of contradictory
elements fused into a sonata
the subtleties *bloodstone agate*
ruby quartz plows under the swamp
thickets grow jailcells cages
blacker than an eclipse of stone
Manwoman I bring forth my lizard
repeating the endless series of
circles the lizard leaps into
my mouth and escapes carrying
my voice to the

>   *wind*
>   *rain*
>   *sun*

❧

He gives me fruit. Lemons tangerines bananas melons. His wings
spattered with moonlight. Taking me inside his stomach full of juices:
birdsong in a storm of flutes. *Peacock blue magenta fuchsia limegreen*
salmon black.

The fruit is good.

෯෮

Your eyes: filters of smoke deepening thickly the ominous chaos of this illusion. I ask myself, why so fearful? Chaos......confusion. Muddled in my own sensitivity. The room softens—each object at once harsh and threatening—transforms. I see you, your eyes sweeping away falling into the chorus of love.

෯෮

We travel in a panther's stomach. Riding for days passing through villages farms forests saints on their way to Hell with thick beards of ivy-tangled words floating between their mouths matted with holiness. A moth trapped inside. I try desperately to shake it through the layers of silk. It flutters and dies while its new wings glisten with coats of lacquer and slobber minutes ago mummified in its cocoon waiting for its gauzy wings to shine melt under the sun's rays. This moth trapped inside the panther

> dead
> for
> lack of sun
> lack of air.

> The moth
> smothered in love.

ও

His penis
flower
of flowers

>Indigo
>cotton
>ears of corn
>morning glories
>sunflowers
>the Ivory Coast

The men paint themselves with rushes
to attract the wind
each layer of
pink
yellow
burgundy
indigo

>a net painted with rain

ও

His penis

a flower blooming in
dark mirrors
Yellowred

its mothy odor rises inside
a frosted circle

Geraniums nasturtiums grape-ivy
pour from its tip

The men grease themselves
with berries
turning their skin
purple and black

Gumming
their hairy thighs with
hashish and opium

The panther falters at the garden pool. Goldfish reflected in his eyes
dart out then in panging with fear. I want to touch him. I want to
heal wounds. I see only my own crystal, my own shattering against
the torrent of the whirlpool. Down down I am pulled into the mass
of weeds. I throw up my hands and grasp the rushes the cattails. The
panther's sleek torso trembles milkweed in a snow storm. I forget myself
give the goldfish sunshine water algae fruit refusing to die grasping life
with fertile hands pushing into the deep well of love. The panther slits
me from neck to navel and begins to chewspit chewspit necklaces of
pearl into my groin. I swell in water lifting my eyes to the wind the
rushes. *Indigo purple burgundy.* I touch his eyes.

❧

Beads collected in a pool
I come like orchids in a field
White mahogany
my garnet skin stacked beside the fire
Stripped
I envy nothing but a wild rain of stars
upon the palm of space

❧

You tell the story of your emotions. I do not know you, you say. I cannot
know you. The you I see is not the you which is you. The you which you
have known for your lifetime. The you I see is the you of Now. What
is your Now, is yourself, transforming. We live in a mirror. I see your
reflection in my own. Never ourselves
but what we see in each other. The mirror's white teeth creating images
of hand-to-hand....the laid-back motion of our bodies.

❧

If whiskers grow straight on the mountains
when the tremors kiss
I will know you

❧

Submergences

Men surround me with tongues of fire. They shout garbled idioms into the air. Daisies! As the tension builds, skyscrapers exPLODE! Farms exPLODE! Sexes EXplode! Nothing is the same. I finger a crimson lute, all eyes upon me. I faint, singing to *Hermaphroditus Uroboros Gorgon Quetzalcoatl Tiamat.*

℞

We set ourselves to task. Four of us form a square, an easily constructed, easily destroyed, grouping of men. Fragile. Mummified in foil. Reflecting the burns.

℞

Inside the square we draw intersecting lines of diagonals. Some men enter the box and surround it. Extending the diagonals, they create two large triangles that lessen the descent of water. Fanning of flames. We appear as two wings of a kite balanced, beautiful infinitely unstable. Eager to change in wind.

℞

Each man enclosed in the womb. The furnace quiet.

℞

One man
narrower through the thighs
Purple

spread over it all

The leafy heads of
emerald-eyed
blackberry bushes
Molten rock
to the level of the trees

Inside was even more

We have soldiers who go
to save a tiny fish:
the shape, musky hailstones
beneath the earth's crust

Lichens grow on infants
All emotion
wounded
from zero to sixty in an elegant maroon
of space into a
mouth and dropped away as if dead

The physical body
you enter
silver-backed
staccato

Water: a hand of liquid beauty. Silk-wrapped, mummified in foil, the bodies eat at each other. I fear the light which smothers dark, carrying each layer of words deeper into the thrust my wound lays open. Water eats at fire. Fire eats at sky. Sky trembles and screams crumbling toy blocks into liquid sediment.

৵

When I awake, I discover a small star-shaped tattoo on my left cheek. Barely perceptible from my olive skin, it vibrates against my seeing it. One moment it is there, the next it seems only a slight flaw in the skin.

By afternoon, it becomes bright scarlet. By nightfall, a deep thick magenta. I feel no pain, but some transformation overcomes me.

৵

When from the corona

          soft

    you pour your dire flame

Eruption

      a mountainous geography

     enters my mouth

We

    the obscured elements

compose a spiralling

         of flesh

seven times

the world's length and breath

Into the abrupt sentence
gasp
and call from the Above
the soul-creature
Corona

At our green roots
bowls
shiny filmy tendrils
ooze out their glass
to attraction's poles now stretch
their dun hairs
by love possessed

Mitered and uncorrupt
I
the plucked
damson
your terrible embrace exposes

Name me One
an exile from the body-prison
into soul-stuff strung

ℜ

Singing a lark
caught in a deep well
throttled heaping wind
through pipes of water
piercing barriers of stone

out into the sunlit world

I cry

೪ტ

When the day grows dark, I sift slowly through galaxies and nebulas. Unbound my earth. A golden bar upon which I lean.

೪ტ

Note: Italicized words are chanted.

Echo

The mirror is where it all begins.

It hung on a green wall for months—old, and tall, and narrow—before I noticed anything.

It was implacable in its finish. The glass was so smooth: a rectangular pool of uncertain depth. The slick, reflective surface like a body of water unstirred by submarine motion: no great predatory fish, no snakes or grinning crocodiles, just the relentless silvery images tossed back at us with a certain insolence. The carved wooden frame glowed gilded and knotted: vines and, at each corner, a horned, grinning face, lolling tongue out as if to drink from the shimmering surface with an ornamental nonchalance. But things were disturbed, finally.

The peculiarities began with a small, framed photograph on a console table behind the couch, an image of a friend—Adrian—and I sharing a weekend in New York. It's a silly photo of the two of us leaving one of the last porn theatres in the city, barely a year before they all closed, before they vanished, ghostly and forever. That was a few months before Adrian too disappeared to parts unknown.

We are dizzy, holding an open book before us, pointing at something in it. An acquaintance that'd traveled with us—and whose name I've since forgotten—took the shot. We are captured a little after

Adrian snuck up on me in the men's room. I remember his face heaving into the glass in which I was running my fingers through my messy hair. It all—after all—begins with a mirror.

Adrian and I are laughing in the picture. We had spent the whole afternoon in the darkened hall, watching pink flesh flicker across the screen... and flash among the shadowed rows of seats, the aisles and the stairwells, each step sticky, crowded with gloom. We were quiet during our tenure in the movie hall, but we are laughing, afterwards.

Today, staring again, I come to my senses for a second and look behind me at the actual photograph whose mere reflection I encounter in the glass. It is the same holiday snapshot on the table, but we are laughing at a closed book. The silver world of the mirror is different, as it must be, however partially.

The difference stirs memory. I recall Adrian hissing at me in the darkness, whispering about his headache. He wanted to go home, and didn't. He complained, I commiserated. We stifled a laugh then, because neither of us would make the slightest move to leave the cinema, a throbbing in the head or no. We spent the whole afternoon in there. I want to say together, but most of the time we vanished, happy, from each other's sight in quest of handsome strangers. He caught me in the men's room though. I remember that, his face hovering over my shoulder as I pushed my fingers through my—suddenly—messy hair. And a few short months later, he vanished from my life.

I remember the film playing on the screen as I sat in the dark. An impossibly handsome man cruising a bright street, Tee shirt peeled off, hung over one shoulder. He, why not call him Angel, struts across a pavement scintillating with heat, the sweat lending him light too.

Angel stops on a corner, lifts his hand to his forehead, scans the passing traffic and leans against a tree. A tall palm takes all his light and drapes him in feathering shadow. It highlights his body. Great plastrons of pectoral muscle are etched with lines of black. A long, white car slows before him and he gets in. The driver and he make a pair. The pair makes idle talk; their hands wander; beneath the pale, worn denim of his jeans his cock hardens visibly, strains at the seam.

In a strange cut away, the dashboard clock flips digital minutes over. Twelve. Thirteen. The soundtrack mangles melody and a clearer, fleshly sound joins it.

A tanned hand slides up and down Angel's erection. Root to glistening glans.

Then his face fills the screen, eyes shut, mouth slightly open, lips bright with saliva. The camera shows us the rear view mirror. It's always about the mirror. Again and again and—in the other glass before me—a shift in my posture unleashes light, obliterating half the image. My eyes shudder, shift, scramble trying to track the remnants of vision. Why do I stare into it at so much length? One of the horned heads in the corners seems to mock me now, tongue out.

His cock curves in the hollow of a hand as the car plunges into violent daylight and expansive blacktop.

The pair arrives at his apartment. The man who drove is darker, slightly taller. One hand cups the denim crotch again, and the other slides up the naked torso to grab at Angel's stubbled chin. They kiss, wetly. A long time. The dark man pushes Angel to his knees. His dress slacks are tenting a few inches below the belt.

In the mirror, in the darkened theater, on the screen, in the room where I believe I am standing. Music plays at a low level. Grows.

Angel sucks at the man. The man beside me in the dark grins and I respond. Strong digits rise to the back of my own neck—burning—in the hall of moving images, pull me down. The Angel vanishes. It is dark again; my face buried in shadows, my mouth suddenly full and only taste and smell signifying and this man's hardness. Until I rise, sight means nothing. A memory.

When I do rise, the dark man is done with the Angel; he exits a shower. He towels off, puts some product in his hair. He leaves the bathroom nude, the tube of hair gel still in his hand, a curious detail. He puts the tube down on a low table covered with post cards. Jumbled among the mix of iconic or lesser-known landmarks and self-conscious camp is one image the camera lingers on a beat too long. A carnival winds its way through a narrow street. Half naked men wear huge planets on their heads that crack open to release—doves, balloons, exploding clouds of glittering paper. There are horses fronting the crowd, caparisoned with tinted sprays on brows. Everyone's mouth is frozen; open in an endless shared laughter, like Adrian and mine, their bodies jumping to an absent music, their clothing shining in a light that is different from the buildings outside. But not more beautiful. The tops of the buildings are as red as alchemist's gold. I hold my breath, and let it out again.

The man beside me, nameless, with strong digits, whispers a "thank you," smiles, teeth bright in dark. Unexpectedly, leans forward to kiss me on the cheek before leaving. The small courtesies of the court of shadows unfolding in the glass. Relentless, I hear the word make its way to me.

The apartment on the screen reminds me of something—a circus tent or a cell in a well-lit monastery—something that we want to find a miracle in. Just past all the expected furniture—the ample sofa, the coffee table and the books—in a corner, is a colony of plants, their baroque greenery and tiny purple flowers spilling out of the place assigned to them and threatening to seize a little too much space.

I lean back in dark and notice a door across the mediated room. A tall narrow mirror, framed golden foliage and fauns, like mine, waits in the projected color and shade. Reflected in the centre of it, at about eye level, is an illustration under glass. It depicts a strange, spiraling shape in blue and green and purple. From the edges grow other, smaller, spirals in similar colors that spawn again and turn until they meet the limits of the frame to disappear, gone somewhere else. They flutter, these shapes, their hues mottled and opaque. They breed new images. They escape. Briefly, a memory of a black bird that circled in the sky as I was sprawled across a lawn comes back. This weird image reflecting in that mirror, hanging on some unseen wall, reminds me of others I have seen, that gorgeous pull and ebb. Seen in books about fractal geometry. They all start with a mirror too.

Strange attractors, I remember only the phrase—the last of the light long gone now. Strange attractors broken down in an otherwise civil phase space pulling flows around with them. Water—asteroids—attention. The single new element in a closed system that ends its regularity.

A lit cigarette unleashes chaos in the cinema, in the room where I stand gazing into mirror, at a reflected picture of that cinema, where I saw a mirror, where I gave a stranger head and Adrian whispered to me in the dark about the curious book he bought. Adrian whispering in the obscurity, about his headache and his desire to leave.

And he did leave, months later, vanishing utterly. Nobody knew where he went, thought for the longest time occasional emails would arrive describing adventures in pursuit of the monstrous that seemed to cavalcade across Eastern Europe. Werewolves and vampires and ghouls, oh my.

Adrian whispering from obscurity again.

Strange attractors, I remember only the phrase—the single new element in a closed system that ends its regularity. And at that very thought, the lights flash for a second, in the room with the mirror, in the cinema, in the framed photo in the mirror on the screen, in the memory, in the whole gorgeous, tenuous, breathless, creaking, gilded, dizzy, massive imperfection of the ever-spreading continuum of all possible worlds, they flash, brilliant, fiery, obliterating sight—all of it this time—nothing but expansive blanching, then go out for a second, only to come back on. A sudden burst of illumination with a life span briefer than a mayfly's. Small irony. Slight violence and then nothing.

Then the cinema, its blackness, the murmuring and slippery sound of flesh met odd to me, disconcerting. I felt myself sharing Adrian's headache, his nervousness, and his eagerness for light though none was present to beckon any longer. Angel walks off the screen, the lover he was with begins to stroke his cock. A white car drives backwards and a man kisses me on the cheeks, says "thank you," sits down beside me, Adrian vanishes, pulls out a book, points to a story about travel, about mirrors and disappearances. I take a seat and stare into a mirror, seeing the image of my empty room, its spartan furniture, the heap of unwashed shirts that clutters up a corner.

And as I sit there a murmuring begins. It seems to come from everywhere at once, but I can't be sure. A soft, vast susurration that pours from the shelves... like all the voices on the screen and in the darkened room began speaking at once, whispering things. I could make out certain words; "satiety," "absence," "pinnacle." As the moments tick by I hear whole sentences—discourses even, which I am not ready to repeat. Then a fiercer noise. A great, heavy knocking from the screen before me, or the space between the screen and I, that throws me off completely. A booming, hollow sound, almost frightening, that makes me want to turn and run through the slim rectangle of light at the end of the darkened hall, signifying "door."

In the men's room I stare into the mirror. I feel like Edward Kelley looking for the spirits. And I feel like I will feel like that for days to come, as I gaze and see nothing but the room, the chair, now vacant, the piles of clothes, the bookcases, the door to the outside world. I am gone, vanished from that hoary space, absent save in the photographic trace from one lost weekend.

I turn from the display. Behind me, there on the console table— once more—are Adrian and I, smiles overbroad and an unconscious pleasure apparent in us—everywhere. The plate glass of the movie house's entrance is still behind us, but the book whose open rows of type stirred us to laughter is closed now, shut against the frozen light, only its jacket displayed to the world. On the cover, I see the same curious pattern, the spiraling shape in blue and green and purple. From its edges grow other, smaller, spirals in similar shades that spawn and turn until they meet the jacket's limits and disappear, gone somewhere else.

I feel my damp eyes widen. I spin around in my seat to look behind me. The room reflected, every bit of furniture in place, an empty chair. I peer through the mirror's gilded frame whose mocking faces I cannot see from my position here, inside. Just the lolling tongues, lapping at me. I am gone from the chair. And the volatile photograph shows an open book. Inside. Outside. The click of the lock turning over. The creak of hinges and across the living room, past the alcove, I see the shape of Adrian shutting the door behind him, his long black trench coat dirty at the hem. He walks past the glass and into the kitchen like he has never been away. Like he lived in this apartment. More spacious than where I am now. Where I'm feeling very cold. It all begins with the mirror. And it all ends there, with Adrian passing by, eyes turned. Eyes turned.

Rome Adventure

Kevin Killian

An American couple in Rome, childless, well-to-do, bored. The auto accident had embittered him, and they had come away from New England to recuperate his sagging spirits. He was writing a horror novel, and she was soaking up the sun on a series of villa patios, tall cool drinks at her fingertips. His novel was called *The Devil You Know*. It took place after a strange virus had invaded the US, leaving its victims (who comprised 90 per cent of Americans) helplessly blind, with fingers growing out of their eye sockets and little eyeballs growing out of their wrists. The fingers couldn't see, and the eyeballs in the wrists glared furiously at the ends of arms, like the daiquiris and Manhattans the writer's wife wore at the end of hers. She suffered herself from Epstein-Barre virus—she felt tired all the time and sometimes could hardly bear to roll over.

Her name was Anna Lacey. To help her dress and apply sunscreen and to mix her drinks, the Laceys had hired a maid who hardly knew a word of English. The maid, who answered to the name of "Lina," lived in a room of her own down the hall from Anna Lacey's, but close enough to hear her name if Anna found the energy to call it out. At other times, she was summoned to Anna's bedside by a portable beeper which she disliked wearing, fearing it to be a work of the devil. Since she further believed that Anna's disease was a religious punishment on her, she was constantly jittery and prayed often, to a crucifix in her air-conditioned bedroom. The day that Joe Lacey had given her the beeper, and haltingly explained its use, Lina had unwrapped it carefully, then with a little scream she took it from it silver-paper box, dropping it on the carpet as though it burned her fingers. Joe told her to wear it on her belt like a rosary. But it was no rosary, it talked in Anna Lacey's voice, whispery, evocative, shrill. "Lina, get me a drink," it said, and Lina had to jump. Another time it told her to make all the beds in the house even though they were all made, except of course for the one where Anna lay at that very moment. Lina stared at the beeper and watched it quiver with its talking. "You'd think she never saw a TV before," Anna said impatiently once, after Lina had displayed her rejection of the beeper by hurling it into the villa's swimming pool. "Doesn't she know it's just like a TV except smaller and with no picture?"

"Then by the same token you're a TV star," Joe said, "and maybe she's never known a star close-up."

"Oh, Joe, that was a low blow," Anna said, referring to her onetime career as a talk show hostess on Italy's number one TV channel, RAI. She had interviewed prominent politicians and authors, and that was where she had met Joe, who sat facing her on camera pushing his new novel *Feeding,* and after a few questions about his book she had decided then and there to quit her job and marry this man, this strange, man with the coal-black eyes and the livid scar across his forehead like the mark of Cain. So after a few months' honeymoon in Boston, they had settled down happily to a life of writing in Rapallo—well, more or less happily, until this disease had struck.

It came on slowly at first—Anna noticed her reading glasses slipping down her nose one day, resolved to get them fixed the next time she went to town, and that was that. The next evening, while making a cocktail for herself, the ice cubes melted in her hands. Her hands were feverishly hot. This was about the same time the Anita Hill-Clarence Thomas confirmation hearings in Washington. On the radio an announcer from the Socialist party was speculating on Thomas' future. When Anna went to lower the volume, the radio short-circuited and began to smoke and fume, and the knob fell off in her hand. The doctor eventually told her this kind of thing was only to be expected for one in her condition, and yet unexpected as well— "You never know what will happen next, with Epstein-Barre," he said. Some complain of cold, some of heat, some gain weight, some lose, but everyone complains of the fatigue. We live in a sunny, peaceful land, it goes with the territory."

Joe scoffed at the village explainer. Had his own surgeons flown in from Boston. Experts all, they confirmed the original diagnosis.

After a bit it seemed clear that, until the virus passed out of Anna's body, there was nothing for her to do but lie there and take it. Joe was sympathetic, but Anna was beginning to feel like a millstone round his neck. Idly she thought of suicide, but decided that her impulse towards self-destruction might, after all, very well be the work of the Devil, and as such had better be avoided for the good of what soul she might still have left after a lifetime of office parties, affairs with RAI executives, a cocaine and alcohol dependency problem that remained unlicked, and marriage to America's #1 horror novelist. Still she fretted that she wasn't ever to get well again, and some days she could hardly dial the sleek Italian modernist phone to talk to the pharmacist or to any of her girlfriends. Then she really felt abandoned, since Joe was increasingly occupied with his dark visions, and Lina grew day to day more afraid and contemptuous both of Anna and of her beeper.

One day she made up her mind. She put aside her drink and tried to sit up in her lounge chair. On the smooth glass top of a table she kept a telegraph pad and, ripping off a yellow sheet, she scrawled a note to the best friend, Giselle, in New York. "Cara, come at once," she wrote. Daily at three in the afternoon a boy bicycled from town to pick up her telegrams and deliver the mail. Today at three she kept him waiting while she fiddled with the wording. From the next room, Joe's study, his typewriter pounded furiously, pouring out like Chianti the reams of words that kept him afloat. He was using her illness; it was all so clear, now that she'd had this inspiration to cable Giselle, and now that she found herself almost unable to compose a decent imperative in any of the languages she and Giselle made themselves clear in when they must. The room was hot. Above her blonde head a fan whirled aimlessly, at low enough a speed that it wouldn't faze the fuses. The Villa had only been wired for electric in the late 50's. Lina was forced almost daily to replace burnt fuses in the damp, chilly cellar, piled with empty bottles of rum and Scotch, through which she'd cleared a path to the gray box that hung on an otherwise empty stone wall.

Lina set out for a walk along the beachfront. She removed her heavy black cape, then her thin bodice, lastly her cheap brown cotton undershirt and walked topless like all the women on the beach. Her silver cross dangled between the breasts the Devil had sent her to torment men with. One man sitting on a toppled flagpole waggled his tongue her way in a lewd way and touched his thumb to his fingertips, loosely rolling his fist in his lap as she walked by. Once they fell into conversation, Lina found he was not so bad. He had a mother and two sisters living in Rapallo, though he himself was just visiting the beachfront area. One of his uncles was a parish priest in the mountains. His name was Vincent, and Lina told him all about Anna and Joe Lacey.

His eyes glittered in the sun as he listened to her story, listened with a queer intensity that kept her talking until she had exhausted her material, and when she had done her tongue felt like a big cock in her mouth. He drew back, hands on knees, and breathed a solitary syllable that frightened her—she knew not what it portended.

It wasn't that he was a bad boy, Lina reflected, just a greedy one. Vincent took her hand and silently led her down the beach to the underside of a rock, where they made love in the cool shadow. "Mother of God, have I spoken too much? Qualms assail me." Spent, Vincent lay gasping in the pool shallows like a fish. Lina watched him, with a combination of fear and tenderness, passing her hand along his loins. She told herself not to fret. "I have qualms, so? Why, even the old get qualms. Age spares no one the heeby jeebies."

Giselle sat wearily slumped in first class, Pan American Flight 202 to Rome. She didn't know why she hadn't just told Anna Lacey to forget it. Whatever else Giselle was, she was not Anna Lacey's maidservant to be summoned from continent to continent the way she was used to shuffling Lina from room to room. Giselle felt more than a little sorry for Anna's long-suffering maid. And only Giselle, out of all the people in the world, was doing anything to help Lina out. For tucked away in her luggage was a magic scapular, blessed by the Cardinal of New York, to help Lina ward away the evil spells created by living in the same house as Joe Lacey. "What is this, my child?" asked the Cardinal gravely. She explained that her best friend was married to Lacey, whose books the Cardinal knew by reputation. She asked the Cardinal if Lacey could somehow have sold his soul to the Devil for popular success.

"It's possible," he agreed, but she detected a reservation in the way his eyes passed over her face sorrowfully. "It is hardly likely, though. The devil exists, yes, but he has other work to do. He finds plenty of work today in my native land, fair Nicaragua."

She brushed away fair Nicaragua like a pesky mosquito. "Well, at least you admit it's possible!" she cried out. "Father, bless this scapular, help one maid defend her soul against perdition. I'm only a New Yorker, I don't know much about your ancient mysteries of salvation. But what I know I know! Anna has changed, Father. When we first met, she was vibrant, alive, magnetic; the most vivacious girl in Europe. Now she's just like a hull or peapod and sits all day knitting and drinking. They claim it's physiology, that it's Epstein-Barre, but isn't it just a little coincidental she didn't come down with this so-called disease till she married Joe Lacey? It's a house of darkness, Your Holiness. Bless this thing, please! I'm imploring you as one good Catholic to another who's high up." Finally he relented and shut the sliding wooden partition gently in Giselle's thankful face.

The Cardinal left the confessional, sunk in thought, and once back in his Residence, picked up his private phone and dialed the number of Brentano's.

"Brentano's, may I help you?"

"This is Cardinal Ramirez at St. Patrick's Cathedral."

"Oh, yes, your Holiness...how may we help you?"

He placed an order for one copy each of the novels of Joe Lacey. The clerk promised to have them sent by UPS to his Residence just as soon as they were packed. Then the Cardinal replaced the receiver and sat back and sighed. On the wall above his breviary a thoughtful housekeeper had placed a handtinted photo of Managua, his birthplace some seventy-five years ago. Since that date much water had flowed under some pretty rickety bridges,. Now his country was once more engulfed in a terrible civil war. With the quick association of ideas critics had remarked in his poetry, Cardinal Ramirez thought again of the soignée red-headed

Giselle, and her strange story of Satanic possession in Rome. He scoffed at such an idea, but in his heart of hearts he knew,—who knows?

When Giselle landed at the airport in Rome, neither Joe nor Anna Lacey was there to meet her plane. Instead they sent Lina and Vincent. Giselle took Lina into the TWA ladies' room and gave her the magic scapular, telling her to wear it next to her heart at all times. Then she excused herself, went into a toilet stall, and snorted some rock cocaine up her nose. Over the metal partitions she heard Lina cry out again and again, "Thank you, Giselle Watson," "Thank you, Signora!" But she hardly heard her, she was in ecstatic white heaven, snow falling from the high, high ceiling and she, shivering, afraid, banging her head on the dispenser for the rough, abrasive toilet paper of Rome. "Thank you, mamma Watson! Blessed be your daughters and sons!"

Paris Over Paris (2002 + 1996 + 2002)

Rob Stephenson

Neither boy is wearing a shirt. The one on the sofa has dark hair and the other one sits awkwardly beside him on the carpet. They stare at each other. The carpeting is a darker red than the sofa. Litter is strewn everywhere. A pair of black briefs is draped over the arm of the sofa. It looks like an advertisement to me, but there is no text that I can see from where I'm standing. Emerging from the soft metallic blue darkness, a large school of fish floats midair as if underwater. One of them is close. An open mouth. I want to put my finger in it. "Soil me," he said so softly I could barely hear him, "please." His little black eyes burned. I wonder if he learned English from the British. Now some of the fish are above me. I see their white underbellies. They are skewered with metal rods that are attached to a black rectangular structure, but a few of them look like they are floating freely without anything holding them in place. Behind the sofa the leaves on the trees are burnt orange. It's cheap wallpaper. The guy at the market gave me a perfect mango and some huge purple grapes and picked some coins off the palm of my hand. Why is it so frustrating for some people when they can't see the whole thing, when it's just a bunch of fragments? And when is it ever more than fragments really? I wonder who keeps the complete ones at home. Hard peaches and nectarines. The colors have darkened. They spend a lot to protect stolen objects. A piece of heavy paper is framed on an easel. A thin rectangle of gold runs through the middle of the wood frame. The easel is the color of fresh pecans, crushed. There is a label at the bottom of the easel, but I can't tell if it's the title of the drawing. The sketch is unfinished. Probably the bare bones conception for a larger work that was never made. Outlined simply in charcoal are a group of centaurs holding a nude Christ-like figure. Straight vertical lines reach upwards to the top of the paper. Trees. Without leaves. Just outside the restaurant. Full moon. Rude waiter. Couscous. He sliced a row of small crescents in the paper tablecloth with the tip of a serrated knife. An ice skater. Or a Chinese calligrapher making a brush stroke. Large nose. Small catalog. Origami ears. He brought yogurt and an apple. Euphoria in little disposable glass jars. Sugar syrup in mint tea afterwards. A delicate mix of intimacy and powerlessness. A man lies on his back on an aquamarine park bench. He is asleep. The bench is designed so that the curving slats comfortably hold four sitting people. Behind the bench is a gray metal fence. It protects a bed of pink flowers, the pink of a little girl's pajamas. The man's hair is long and dirty, pushed back from his forehead and hanging off the front of the bench. The skin of his face is sunburned and unwashed. Dirt has been collecting in layers for days. His mouth is half-open, as if he's waiting to be kissed. I can't tell if he has any teeth. He clutches himself in a loose hug. I wonder what his mouth tastes like. There are men in nearby apartments looking out over the window grills and smoking cigarettes. My parents pushing me along the burlesque streets of New Orleans when I was ten. A praline sticky in my hand. Latin words in gold on marble. A city full of theories. Side by side. The timid joy of thinking useless things. Stratified pastries about to be folded inside floral printed wax paper. I see a courtyard through six windowpanes. The upper left pane is slightly opaque with age, while the other five panes are warped and distort the view of the courtyard and the building across the courtyard. There is a clock that says three minutes after four. Mid-morning light bathes a triangular bed of tulips in full-Spring bloom. One of the windows of the building across from me has closed chalk-green draperies. The rest have flimsy white curtains. Behind me, between an Italian globe, brown with age, and an open book with very tiny hand-written letters, I hear whispering that sounds like a simmering stew. As I walk away past the long silent tables, a section of the card catalog opens and a middle-aged woman walks out from a room I had no idea was even there. This time without sugar. I ordered a quick espresso with a spot of froth. I sat down on an oak chair between mirrors framed in baby blue and a grown-up shade of maroon. They were slanted in such a way that reflected the white-hot noonday. My own glances were returned on every side. I savored my own quiet attention, my casual inspections. My heart pounded. There were bags of rubbish so carefully arranged on the curb outside. The waiter brought me a plate of strawberry sorbet surrounded by a dense meringue set amidst a drizzle of lemon-raspberry syrup and mint leaves. "...delightful creature," a young man says in broken English to a scabby girl half his age as he walks by the open window, "but trapped in a menagerie of his own time." Above his gruff voice, the gentle river of French voices in the café flow just outside my daydreams. It's as if their mouths are full of oily marbles. Mostly it is some kind of lettering that is unrecognizable to me, except for a distinct red dollar sign that has been spray-painted in thicker strokes than the rest of the graffiti. Halfway down the concrete steps is a short break in the stairway, a level area with two flat trapezoidal stones that sit on top of the concrete instead of being imbedded in it. Next to the stones is a patch of miniature round stones that are set in the concrete in an uneven grid pattern. I knew I wouldn't come back to this place. I didn't want to see him again. But I did like him better after he said he was not happy and it was impossible for him to buy anyone water. I even liked his girlfriend who told me, "Black and white is only in the movies." I fingered the foil-wrapped mint chocolate in my shirt pocket I'd bought earlier to eat on the Metro. As I walked off, he called after me, " I'm just dying to see the inside of a fancy Parisian apartment." I can see a desk against the far wall. Who would leave the door to a place like this open? There are a dozen orange roses fanning out in a white vase. They appear more yellowish where the light from the window hits them. The view out the window is of a balcony across the courtyard. It's full of plants. A man in a gray sweatshirt is watering them with a hose. He is looking down at some red flowers, a variety that I don't recognize. His head is shaved. He has no idea that I am taking his photograph. To the right of the window above the desk is a wall. Paint that was once white is curling downward in thin ribbons. An oval mirror with a mahogany frame reflects a few windowpanes, but nothing is reflected beyond the glass from outside the room except a milky whiteness. "It's just too convenient for some people to be stupid," a voice said behind me. A woman's voice. Spanish. The doors shut automatically, but it felt so different from the subway in New York. The boy standing next to me kept feeling his neck with long fingers and long nails. He touched his lips a lot. He was restless in his own body, reminding me of a fidgeting baby rat. His pants were riding so low on his hips that I wished his shoes were untied, but like mine, his sneakers had no laces. They were slip-ons. "Liebhaber," the tattoo said in a monstrous font across the small of his back. He had big feet. Beef. Uncooked with raw chopped onion and a dish of mysterious green leaves sautéed and fragrant. One custard fruit tart and after that, another. I hear accordion and violin struggling for a blend. It makes the music sad. I enjoy it more than the second tart. And

I realize that the shadows forming and dissolving behind the shade across the air well last night, were made by two people holding candles as they moved around the room. When they blew them out, I saw the little red glow of their cigarettes. Almost touching. A black dog comes up to me as I sit down on a bench. He licks melted mint chocolate off my fingers. The swarthy man in the shadows whistles sweetly and the dog runs off mid-lick. Midnight. Not quite rain. Sumptuous yellow curry sauce on my tongue. Wonderful old cameras and kinescopes in an unlit shop window. A boy in a bubble-gum pink polo shirt on a street full of whores. I cried into the goose-down pillow the same way I had when I was watching the sunset paint the cathedral and the river. Oh shit, I really am a tourist. Trick mirrors. Magic boxes. The smell of his chest and the feel of the stiff hairs there tickling my ear. Hiding my wet face inside a jewel. Images of black men spread out on the tables and on the walls. Everyone sits quietly watching porno instead of each other. I am completely alone in a room full of men who are too private about their own desires while someone else's flicker across their faces. Outside. In the dark by the river. I pay attention to how the rain on my head changes every few moments and how it doesn't quite correspond to the patterns it makes on the street's puddles. There was a man here earlier dipping his fingers in glasses of water and rubbing them on the rims. He made long droning tones that never quite repeated themselves. What if you had to pay admission to go outside? And no elevators. Two different kinds of cheese every day for weeks and never having the same kind twice. During the meal I watch her hands. They did things to make you look at them. Fingers rubbing together. Digital frottage. Poses and perfect motion. A balanced economy. Holding the fork just so. The plane's wheels made curly clouds of blue-gray smoke that the body of the plane passed through and left behind. Another brush stroke of the calligrapher. There is a scene of brown bears framed in red with little white light bulbs that are not lit. Underneath, a child with long brown hair and a dark blue jacket sits on a giraffe. A girl? I can only see the back of the child's head. A boy sits on an ostrich. He looks back at the other child. A lion stands between them and as the music starts they all spin out of sight. Next to the Ferris wheel everyone stops speaking. They turn to look at me and then continue eating, carefully, as if they might hurt the food if they hurried or had any aggression toward it whatsoever. Thick copper poles run vertically between the shoulder blades of many white horses. Their ears are flat and their mouths are gasping for breath. They could be in agony. They shine. I want to touch them. Their legs are bent as if they are galloping. But they remain still. They all have horseshoes on their upturned hooves. There are no children in sight. Tan saddles and bridles adorn the horses, but they are not identical on every horse. One has a pink blanket rolled up at the back of the saddle. Another has a yellow blanket unrolled and hanging down its side. Carnival-colored feathers and tassels ornament their bodies. Plastic or painted wood? His pale arms pick up the lime green light from overhead. Eighteen? And so drunk. He dropped his box of cigarettes on the floor between my legs and looked at me as he bent down. Twice in a half-hour. I'm so tired of this. Two crows pecking around on the big lawn. Contortionists with bicycles. Some guys doing martial arts routines. I moved away from them. I clutched my shopping bags and lay face down on the grass next to four people playing a card game for small change. I felt safe and dozed immediately to the sound of insects buzzing. Bird wings flapping. The shuffling of the deck. Dusk. Huge bursts of flame flared out of a young man's mouth up into the air. I smelled the heat on my face. I heard bells in the distance and people talking in a language I couldn't identify. I don't want any more crepes on this trip. Back and forth in front of one of the closed stalls. An acrobat with sore nipples. A bit narcoleptic. The crowd watches. Sweat on their necks. A circus that comes out of its own womb. "I'll never do this in public," he said as he spread a vivid red smear across paper. The same color as his lips. I pick at the ham pizza under my fingernails in the taxi back to the apartment. I don't bother to interrupt the driver's crazy rant. Hot baths without soap. Stained glass. A cemetery of terra cotta and old soil. Incomprehensible arches in cracked white stucco.

The Yorkshire Adonis

Shaun Levin

1   I'm leaving you to come back to you. My journeys in the past have always left scorched earth behind them.

2   Almost immediately we became two men writing together in a room; two men alone for so long, with ways they are set in—this could be the start of a lifetime together.

3   That, my mother has said, is the best thing: Having someone to hold you.

4   How close *partner* is to *parent*. The second fits into the first with an R left over. R is the name of my love.

5   Your desire for me is the birth of my self-love, and its sustenance.

6   This morning in my room here, I helped a spider kill a fly by whacking the fly off the window and onto the ledge. The spider darted out from its hole in the wood, bit into the fly's head until the fly buzzed itself to a halt.

7   The aim is to reach a state of joy that is selfish and harmless.

8   Nine times I washed my face in the mirror-river after I got here, then climbed back up onto the path, away from the mystic play of shadows that twined and twisted as if they were alive.

9   With my glasses in my pocket, the world is an impression of greens and light and shade, the path back to the house is cream and white. This is what Monet saw when he thought he was going blind: a haze of greens and purples.

10   The joy is massive, untinged by longing—I am allowed giddy and senseless happiness.

11   Now, away from you, I can write about you. Only two months since we met at Michael's party; far enough for questions other than: Is he the one? Being long-sighted, I can see you better from a distance. And by distance, I mean a four-hour train ride from London.

12   Yorkshire in the summer. Everywhere, daisies draw bees to them.

13

14   When we are excited by ourselves—truly impressed and amused—then we will seduce.

15   The quiet of morning, and always the water from the valley: an

entire stadium of fans cheering in the distance.

16   There's a finch in the bush outside my writing hut; a gulpable little bird bobbing along the fence. It makes me think of the tiny bird one eats whole, blindfolded, the bird that's illegal to kill, the one Francois Mitterand ate two of before he died. They were his last dejeuner.

17   I love domesticity; the theatricality of small gestures: making tea for you, brushing our teeth and flossing, especially flossing, a theatricality that has grown out of years of fantasizing. I'd reached a point where wanting and disappointment were indistinguishable. Domesticity excites me in the same way that all acted-out fantasies feel dangerous and deliciously perverse.

18   I met the Yorkshire Adonis while jogging up the hill yesterday. He knew how beautiful he was and had his T-shirt off and tucked into his jeans. I asked him—it was the first question that came to me—I said: "If I keep running, will I come out the other side?" We smiled while we talked, shy and delighted.

19   Last night I stood facing the valley with my cock out, Adonis at my feet. It was a mild evening, the only sounds were the river, a dog barking near the mill, and voices coming from the garden above me. I had been waiting for this all day. "Suck it," I said. Adonis did everything I told him, until I came on the lawn.

20   Now is the time for grace.

21   Loneliness is no longer my abstract noun of choice; it's not

my constant companion and prod? Once, my loneliness was fatal and reliable, everything began with it. Now I've added moderation, I am not the Shaun they mean when they say: Oh, him.

22   From the garden I called to R, who was about to take his soufflé from the oven: "Babe," I said, "Could you heat up the ratatouille; put it on quite low with the lid off so the water can evaporate." And he said: "Do you want the heat diffuser under it?" And I said: "Yes, yes, I think so." The tones of our voices were gentle, as if our kindness to each other had been consistent for years.

23   Tonight I picked my first raspberry; Adonis showed me how. We walked the garden path by torchlight; him in front, me on an adventure. His childhood, he said, was full of raspberries. I said: "I fed mulberry leaves to silk worms and squashed larvae from their cocoons." He said: "I wish you'd come in my mouth last night." I said: "You know, R and I went to visit Virginia and Leonard last Saturday; their raspberry bushes were old, the fruit neglected." "Look," said Adonis, "I'm about to show you the white phallus of the raspberry, and all you can think about is your boyfriend. It's not attractive." He shines his torch on a raspberry, picks it, and my world expands. This is what Columbus felt when he landed wherever he landed.

24   "It's August in Yorkshire," he says.
        "Prove it," I say.
        "There are leaves on the trees," he says.
        "And?" I say.
        "That's it," he says.

25   This love spreads over my entire body—and by love I mean the desire and the curiosity to know you intimately, and to fuck and be fucked deeply. It spreads over the skin and into every internal organ; not just to the stomach where longing exists or to the fingertips that want to cling.

26   Before coming to Yorkshire, R and I drove from Brighton to Rodmell to visit the Woolfs. "Virginia's out fucking with Vita," Leonard said. He frowned his way around the garden, so R and I collected apples: pink ladies and golden delicious. "The aubergines look gorgeous, Leonard," R. said. "Yes," Leonard said, "Good old aubergines." Dinner was a feast—bangers and mash, with broccoli and peas—and Leonard relaxed a bit, told us about the Horticultural Society he was setting up in the village.

27   Adonis wants me to come back to the farm with him; he says he just bought the new David Hasselhoff CD from the Oxfam shop in Hebden Bridge; he says he has this great Nautilus machine and nipple clamps he wants to show me. I say: "It's starting to rain, I'd better head on home; R is waiting for me with a pesto and polenta soufflé, and the ratatouille is almost done."

28   She says: Excitement is the rising tide of desire waiting for a response from the world.

29   (pause)

30   (pause)

31   Applause.

Contributors

Will Aitken has published three novels—*Realia, A Visit Home* and *Terre Haute*. His writing has appeared in *Paris Review, Threepenny Review* and a variety of other publications in North America and the UK.

"When I write I always try to keep at least one Surrealism in the kennel because it knows the secrets of the deep and it doesn't bark."

Stephen Beachy is the author of the novels *The Whistling Song* and *Distortion* and two novellas, *Some Phantom/No Time Flat*. His latest novel, *boneyard*, from which this story ("Epidemic") is taken will be forthcoming in a couple of years or so, he believes. He is working on a series of essays that explore the relationships between human evolution and various dreamworlds, among other things, and another novel that descends into hell several times, describing the scenery en route. He admires and has been influenced by such writers of the fantastic and grotesque as Julio Cortazar, William Burroughs, Juan Rulfo, Clarice Lispector, Anna Kavan, Kathy Acker, Alvin Lu, Ascher/Straus, Stacey Levine, Can Xue, Jacob Boehme and the Brothers Grimm. Leonora Carrington and Antonin Artaud's descriptions of their own insanity are equally illuminating texts as is *The Autobiography of a Schizophrenic*

Girl. He believes that the relationship between hallucinations and reality is infinitely complex.

Jeffery Beam's *The Beautiful Tendons: Uncollected Queer Poems 1969—2007* is due in June 2008 in the White Crane Wisdom Series from White Crane Books/Lethe Press. His many award-winning works include *Visions of Dame Kind*, *An Elizabethan Bestiary Retold*, and the online book, *Gospel Earth*. The art-song cycle *Life of the Bee*, with gay composer Lee Hoiby, can be heard on Albany Record's *New Growth*. His CD, *What We Have Lost: New and Selected Poems*, was a 2003 Audio Publishers Award finalist. Beam is poetry editor of *Oyster Boy Review* and a botanical librarian at UNC-Chapel Hill, North Carolina. <www.unc.edu/~jeffbeam/index.html>

"Submergences" reflects the early impact of Rimbaud, the Symbolists, Nin, Sitwell, Monique Wittig, and, particularly, French Surrealism, had on my aesthetic [before I came to know Spanish Surrealism, which, too, has left its mark on me.] I believe the subconscious is a beacon from another reality and in the operative conjunction of opposites. Written using automatic writing, "Submergences" narrates an unfolding love which hurled me in my late teens into a Melvillian "Encantada"—a bleakness, a romance, a strangeness, a wild beauty. In these words already throbs the longing for the Divine which stills propels my writing; the struggle to unite the Body and the Spirit into One Knowledge, One Transfiguration. Although pure Surrealism is not a mode in which I now write, it modulates my sensitivities still, and is an undercurrent in my more Objectivist / minimalist current style.

Stephen Boyer: I write surrealism largely because it reflects my experience in the world. I've always been drawn to writer's who feel drawn to the grotesque and the darker parts of humanity; thus the Bataille and Byron references in the piece. They are two of my major literary inspirations because they, like me, seemingly, often look at life from the toilet bowl. I also have work forthcoming in *Cool Thing: Best Gay Fiction 2008*, Blair Mastbaum and Will Fabro, eds. (Running Press, 2008)

Tom Cardamone is the author of the erotic fantasy novel, *The Werewolves of Central Park*. His short stories have appeared in several anthologies and publications. His story here, "Yolk," was a simple exercise; he wanted to write the anatomy of a wet dream.

Growing up on the West Coast of Florida, The Salvador Dali Museum in St. Petersburg was the road trip du jour his high school senior year. If there's such a thing as a gateway drug for Surrealism, Salvador Dali is it. An interest in Dorothea Tanning, Max Ernest and Yves Tanguy followed, the latter's landscape paintings a definite influence on "Yolk." You can read more of Tom's work at his website, www.pumpkinteeth.net.

Sven Davisson is the editor of *Ashé! Journal of Experimental Spirituality* and publisher of Rebel Satori Press. He is author of the collection *The Starry Dynamo: The Machinery of Night Remixed*. He has a degree in Queer Studies and Cultural Theory from Hampshire College. In addition to *Ashé*, his work has appeared in *Abrasax: Journal of Magick and Decadence, mektoub* and *Velvet Mafia*.

Davisson's work is heavily influenced by the collaborative theories of William S. Burroughs and Brion Gysin, the critical meanderings of Michel Foucault, the occult extravagences of Aleister Crowley and the gutter poetry of Marc Almond. He is currently at work on a magickal novel *The Devil's Table*. For more information: www.svendavisson.com

Peter Dubé is a Montréal-based writer and the author of the chapbook *Vortex Faction Manifesto* (Vortex Editions, 2001), the novel *Hovering World* (DC Books 2002) and *At the Bottom of the Sky* (DC Books 2007), a collection of linked short fiction. His fiction deploys dense verbal surfaces to investigate the way narrative shapes our experience of the world, particularly at the points where imagination, desire and the body politic intersect. In addition to his fictional work, his essays and critical writings have been widely published in journals such as *CV Photo, ESSE, Spirale* and *Ashé!* and in exhibition publications for various galleries, among them SKOL, Mercer Union and the Leonard and Bina Ellen Gallery of Concordia University.

His interest in surrealism began in his adolescence, much like his interest in handsome men. He finds it difficult to be sure which has led him to more strange adventures, but happily neither is likely to vanish any time soon. You can visit him online at www.peterdube.com

Craig Laurance Gidney has had fiction published or forthcoming in the following venues: *Spoonfed, Say...Have You Heard This One?, Ashé Journal*, and the anthologies *Magic in the Mirrorstone* and *So Fey*. He lives in his native Washington, D.C.

"The Magus Club" was partially inspired by *Les Chants De Maldoror*, by Lautremont, which is considered the first surrealist text. The bizarre epic prose poem is a masterpiece of nihilism and the grotesque. The imagery of the mysterious Lautremont (or Isidore Ducasse) had and still has a galvanic effect on me. Never has decay and disgust seemed so...beautiful. The novel/poem is a howl against inhumanity; and at the same time, it is about the wisdom of the outsider, and the freak.

I discovered *Maldoror* through my study of the Negritude poet Aime Cesaire, who was deeply influenced and inspired by the Surrealists when he was a student in Paris. Cesaire used the tools and techniques of the Surrealists to explore the colonized psyche. Like the Surrealists, I use fantasy and dream imagery to reveal deeper truths.

Nicholas Alexander Hayes's creative work has appeared in various journals including *Bloom*, *5_trope*, *queerPhilosophy*, *Lodestar Quarterly*, *Eleven Eleven* and *Suspect Thoughts*. He is currently collaborating on queerly contemporary retellings of Greek myths with Terri Griffith. He has always been fond of Duchamp, Bataille, Kharms, and Joseph Cornell; however, Amy England helped him find some reconciliation with Breton.

Trebor Healey is the author of the 2004 Ferro-Grumley and Violet Quill award-winning novel, *Through It Came Bright Colors* (Harrington Park Press, 2003), a book of poetry, *Sweet Son of Pan,* (Suspect Thoughts, 2006), and a short story collection, *A Perfect Scar & Other Stories* (Harrington Park Press, 2007). Trebor lives in Los Angeles, and though he does not always write in a surreal fashion, considers dreams and free association to be his primary means of inspiration and literary liberation. www.treborhealey.com

Kevin Killian, US poet, novelist, critic and playwright, has written a book of poetry, *Argento Series* (2001), two novels, *Shy* (1989) and *Arctic Summer* (1997), a book of memoirs, *Bedrooms Have Windows* (1989), and a book of stories, *Little Men* (1996) that won the PEN Oakland award for fiction. A second collection *I Cry Like a Baby* was published by Painted Leaf Books in 2001. With Lew Ellingham, Killian has written often on the life and work of the US poet Jack Spicer [1925-65] and co-edited Spicer's posthumous books *The Train of Thought* and *The Tower of Babel*. Currently Killian and Peter Gizzi are preparing a new edition of Spicer's collected poetry for Wesleyan University Press.

I remember going to dinner with Denis Hollier and Rosalind Krauss fifteen years ago and thinking, these two are geniuses, but because of my homosexual relativism I know more about surrealism than they do just by the nature of my place in the universe contra theirs; this attack of essentialism was basically gone by the time we got to dessert but tinges of its afterglow remain with me to this day, like lightning bugs leading me down a dark garden.

Shaun Levin's collection of short stories, *A Year of Two Summers*, was published in 2005. A novella, *Seven Sweet Things*, was published in 2003. His stories appear in anthologies as diverse as *Between Men*, *Modern South African Stories*, *Boyfriends from Hell*, *The Poetry of Men's Lives*, and *The Slow Mirror: New Fiction by Jewish Writers*. Shaun is the editor of *Chroma: A Queer Literary Journal* and teaches creative writing in London. See more at www.shaunlevin.com and www.chromajournal.co.uk.

I'm a great believer in the power of automatic writing to pull up gifts from the subconscious. I do most of my initial writing in a cheap spiral-bound notebook that I carry everywhere with me. I try to be uncensored and unjudgemental about those first marks on the page. It's not easy, but when it works, when the images and the truth surprise me, it feels close to a miracle. Breton defined surrealism as "pure psychic automatism"—an act of letting go, of the mind's chaotic order. "The Yorkshire Adonis" came out of a collection of these spontaneous acts of writing: fact mixed with fiction, dead characters with the living,

Katherine Mansfield, and then a beautiful Yorkshire man who came down the hill, jogging in the opposite direction, and transformed into the god.

Rob Stephenson: Though I have read much Surrealist writing, I have always been drawn particularly to the visual art certain artists produced. Marcel Duchamp's exquisite mind, Matta's trance-inducing spatial explorations, Max Ernst's cut and pasted visual novels, Joseph Cornell's charming collage boxes and films are a few of the Surrealist things I treasure. My writing has appeared in all sorts of places online and in print, including: *Entangled Lives, the Mad Hatter's Review, Dispatx, BUTT, Dangerous Families, Skin and Ink, Best Gay Erotica, Best Bisexual Erotica, Black Sheets,* and *Blithe House Quarterly.* I edited the anthology *Tough Guys* with Bill Brent which was nominated for a Firecracker Award. Mikael Karlsson and I made the experimental project *dog*, now out on Please MusicWorks. Listen at www.dog-cd.com.